KU-283-524

ISSUES IN EDUCATION

VOLUME 2

GUEST EDITOR:

ÁINE HYLAND

AS TI
CUMANN NA
MEÁNMHÚINTEOIRÍ
ÉIRE
ASSOCIATION OF
SECONDARY TEACHERS
IRELAND

ASTI Education Journal 1997

Published by ASTI © 1997.

The views expressed in this book are the views
of the contributors and are not
those of ASTI.

No part of this publication may be copied,
reproduced or transmitted in any form or by any
means, without permission of the publishers.

ISBN 1 901852 00 8

Guest Editor: Áine Hyland.
Advertising and Business Manager: Gerry Costigan.
Origination, separations and film: Keystrokes, Dublin.
Front Cover: From a painting by Aidan Powell.
Printing: Brindley Dollard, Dublin.

Contents

This publication has been sponsored by:

**WOODCHESTER
BROKERS**

PREFACE

The ASTI is proud to publish the second issue of its education journal *Issues in Education*. The ASTI which represents 15,300 teachers in second level schools publishes this journal annually to contribute to the public debate on education and its role in our society.

Each issue of the journal takes a major theme and deals with it in an exhaustive manner. The first issue dealt with senior cycle education and the ASTI was very gratified by the response which included many requests for copies from those involved in important decision making positions in education. When consideration was being given to the second issue it seemed logical to take the Junior Cycle as the theme. Junior Cycle education has been undergoing change since 1989 when new Junior Certificate courses were first introduced in a range of subjects. A number of analyses of the Junior Certificate examination results have been carried out by the Educational Research Centre, St. Patrick's College, Drumcondra, and the NCCA is currently engaged in a review of the Junior Certificate curriculum.

The ASTI believes that there is a danger that change fatigue can occur in an education system and that it is important that change should not be "imposed"; it should be measured and should be incremental and accompanied by extensive in career training for teachers. No system can be allowed to stagnate but equally teachers, parents and indeed pupils must be convinced that the change is practical and flexible.

For this second edition of *Issues in Education* the ASTI is privileged to have obtained the services as guest editor of Professor Áine Hyland, one of the most respected educationalists in Ireland. Professor Hyland has experience as a first level, second level and third level teacher. In the past she has been most willing to give of her time and expertise to the ASTI and in agreeing to act as the guest editor of this edition of *Issues in Education* the ASTI is very mindful of the honour which she has bestowed on us.

The ASTI hopes that editions of *Issues in Education* will build up to an authoritative set of volumes to which anybody who wishes to inform themselves about developments in Irish education may refer.

The ASTI would also like to thank Woodchester Brokers for their sponsorship of this publication.

Charlie Lennon
General Secretary

John Mulcahy
President

EDITORIAL BOARD OF THE ASTI EDUCATION JOURNAL:

Officers of the Association
Mr John Mulcahy, President
Mr John Hurley, Vice-President
Mr Tommy Francis, Immediate Past-President
Mr Michael Ward, Honorary Treasurer
Mr Charlie Lennon, General Secretary

Mr Pat Carty, Chairperson of the Education Committee

Ms Dolores Mullins, Chairperson of the Equality Committee

Mr Willie Hallihan, Chairperson of the Principals' Advisory Committee

Mr P.J. Sheehy, ASTI Standing Committee

Ms Irene Irish, ASTI Standing Committee

Ms Ann Walsh, ASTI Standing Committee

GUEST EDITOR'S NOTE

I am honoured to accept the ASTI's invitation to be guest editor of the second issue of the educational journal *Issues in Education*. The inaugural issue which was edited by Pádraig Hogan and published in March 1996, was a great success and was a welcome addition to the somewhat sparse literature on developments in Irish education. This issue focuses on the junior cycle of post-primary education - an area which has seen many changes in the past decade.

The November issue of ASTIR contained an open invitation to teachers to contribute to this publication and I would like to thank the many teachers who responded to the invitation. Teachers are in a unique position, by virtue of the knowledge and experience gleaned in the classroom, to provide an insight into curricular innovation, and opportunities to share these insights are rare. I would also like to thank the other contributors who responded generously and willingly to the request for an article on a pre-determined topic. Many felt that the limit of 2,500 words would be a constraint, but they abided by the parameters laid down thereby making my task as editor a relatively easy one.

As was the case in the inaugural edition, contributors were invited to write in a personal capacity rather than as spokespersons of particular interests or bodies. This allowed individuals to draw from their various experiences while not feeling constrained by existing policy positions. The articles are written from different perspectives and in different styles, and this individuality adds to the richness of the publication.

This journal adds a new dimension to our knowledge of junior cycle developments. It deserves to be widely read by teachers and I hope it will encourage them to reflect further on their own experiences and practices. I would like to express my gratitude to the Editorial Board for their support and advice. I enjoyed editing the journal and I hope the reader will learn as much from this issue as I learned.

Áine Hyland
Education Department,
University College,
Cork.

May 1997.

INTRODUCTION

ÁINE HYLAND

This, the second volume of Issues in Education, focuses on the curriculum at Junior Cycle. As we approach the twenty first century, it is timely to remind ourselves that mass education at second level is a very recent phenomenon. At the turn of the twentieth century, less than one in ten of an age cohort enrolled in a secondary school. As recently as 1963, less than 45% of the relevant age group completed junior cycle education. Many readers of this journal attended secondary school at a time when they were a privileged minority. It is sobering to bear these figures in mind and to realise that this generation of teachers has lived and worked through a period of extraordinary educational change.

Today, there are 375,000 pupils enrolled in second-level schools in the Republic of Ireland, more than 208,000 of them at junior cycle level. Two-thirds of these are enrolled in secondary schools, over 25% in vocational schools and the remainder in community and comprehensive schools. They are taught by a total of more than 20,000 teachers and all follow a broadly similar curriculum leading to the same examination at the end of the three year course. The situation was quite different thirty years ago when there was a clear divide between the curriculum followed by pupils in secondary schools and that followed by pupils in vocational schools. Until the late sixties, vocational school pupils followed a two year course leading to the Day Group Certificate examination and secondary schools pupils followed either a three or four year course leading to the Intermediate Certificate examination. It was not until 1969 that vocational school pupils were permitted to sit the Intermediate Certificate examination and the option of sitting either the Group or the Intermediate Certificate existed until 1991. (In some schools pupils sat the Group Cert at the end of second year and the Inter Cert at the end of third year).

One of the specific terms of reference of the Interim Curriculum and Examinations Board set up by Minister for Education, Gemma Hussey, in 1984 was "to make recommendations regarding a new unified assessment system for the junior cycle of second level schooling, to replace the present Intermediate and Group Certificate examinations". In its discussion paper *Issues and Structures in Education,* the Board highlighted the need for a broader and more balanced core curriculum at junior cycle and proposed a curriculum framework which would consist of a Core which would be obligatory for all pupils and a series of options described as "additional contributions". Following widespread consultation, the framework was modified and in 1986, was presented to the Minister in the report *In Our Schools.* This report emphasised that courses at junior cycle should be designed so as to meet the needs of the entire ability range of pupils and advised that they should be offered at up to three levels - Foundation, General and Advanced. By providing the possibility of offering courses at up to three levels, the Board "was allowing for courses to be designed and taught in accordance with educational objectives and methodologies which are appropriate to the interest, aptitude and achievement of students at each level" and would also help to ensure that "all students may have access to a valid educational experience in each curricular area within the context of a unified system of assessment and certification".

The new Junior Certificate examination programme was introduced by Minister for Education, Mary O'Rourke, in 1989 for all pupils entering second-level schools in September of that year and the first Junior Certificate examination was held in 1992. In *A guide to Junior Certificate* issued in 1989, it was stated that the Junior Certificate programme "draws upon the best and most successful elements of the former programmes for the Intermediate Certificate and the Day Vocational (Group) Certificate", and that the intention of the new programme "is to provide a programme which will encompass those skills and competencies which all young people should have as a right, together with qualities of creativity, initiative and enterprise which are now more than ever so important".

All the articles in this volume refer to aspects of the curriculum at junior cycle, addressing them from a wide range of perspectives. The first article by Pádraig Breathnach provides an overview of the introduction of the Junior Certificate. It outlines the work of the Curriculum and Examinations Board and of its successor the National Council for Curriculum and Assessment. It provides a critique of the new junior cycle programme and focuses particularly on issues relating to assessment. The article concludes by suggesting that while progress in some curricular areas has been limited, the unification of certification systems (Intermediate Cert. and Group Cert.) was successfully achieved.

This is followed by an analysis of teacher development by David Tuohy, with particular reference to junior cycle change. Tuohy's article goes much farther than merely recording the sometimes disappointing approach taken by officialdom to inservice education during the period when new subject syllabi were being introduced at junior cycle in the late 1980s and early 1990s. It provides a theoretical framework and a suggested structure for planning and implementing a teacher development programme and provides a direction for future planning. It argues that what is called for is "a shift to a comprehensive approach, in which a dialogue is opened with the teachers where their real needs are heard and responded to and the needs of the system are shared with them".

The documentation of the CEB and the NCCA had pointed out that curriculum should not be seen as merely knowledge and content. The report *In Our Schools* (1986) defined curriculum as "all those activities which take place within the organisational framework of the schools to promote the development of its pupils" and asserted that "teaching and learning styles strongly influence the curriculum". The White Paper on Education (1995) referred to the importance of active learning methodologies and quoted the Report on the National Education Convention which emphasised "the need for styles of pedagogy which engage and involve all students more actively in the teaching-learning interaction than was traditional." The third article in this collection draws on an innovative and exciting project carried out by the Education Department of St. Patrick's College Maynooth and directed by Jim Callan - the Schools for Active Learning project. The article focuses on issues which militate against effective implementation of the junior cycle curriculum, categorising these issues under two main headings - structural and teachers' values. It concludes that fundamentally, there is a values shift involved in moving to active learning and that this requires deeper appreciation in this country than it has received to date.

The fourth article describes a project currently being undertaken by the

Education Department of University College Cork and directed by Joan Hanafin. This article looks at the implications of Howard Gardner's theory of Multiple Intelligences for Curriculum and Assessment in the Irish context. It discusses changing constructs of intelligence and summarises and critiques Gardner's theory. It addresses a number of questions which arise for teachers who attempt to apply this theory to their classroom practice and states that while a Multiple Intelligences approach calls for a fundamental appraisal/re-appraisal of how we view intelligence and potential in relation to all the pupils we teach, such re-appraisal is within the scope of every teacher and every school. The article concludes by asserting that "Good schools and effective teachers carry out many re-evaluations of their own effectiveness every day. Gardner's theory applied to school contexts provides a flexible and challenging lens through which to conceptualise such ongoing professional acts".

The issue of gender equity has been on the educational agenda in Ireland since the mid 1980s. A comprehensive article by Mary Duggan and Carmel Heneghan looks at gender equity and the junior cycle curriculum under the headings Curriculum Principles; Flexibility; Classroom Interaction; Sexism in Texts; Gender Differences in Subject Choice and Gender Difference in Examination Results. The article expresses disappointment that despite efforts to present junior cycle subjects in a gender friendly manner, there are still considerable gender differences in participation in subjects traditionally associated with gender. The authors suggest that whether gender equality is considered at all in the school and in the classroom depends on the extent to which the principal and staff are conscious of the need for its promotion.

Three articles address, from different perspectives, issues relating to children with special educational needs. Michael Shevlin discusses the integration of children with disabilities into mainstream schools. Anne O'Brien's article refers to second level education for traveller children. Aileen O'Gorman writes about remedial teaching from the point of view of an experienced and practising remedial teacher. The White Paper on Education (1995) sets out government policy on issues relating to children with disabilities and to traveller children. In relation to children with disabilities, it states "the objective will be to ensure a continuum of provision for special educational needs, ranging from occasional help with the ordinary school to full-time education in a dedicated centre or unit, with students being enabled to move from one type of provision to another as necessary and practicable". It identifies a clear target in relation to traveller children stating that "within ten years all traveller children will complete junior cycle education and 50% will complete the senior cycle". Michael Shevlin's article discusses the challenges facing teachers in mainstream schools in their efforts to respond adequately to pupils with special needs in their classes. The article explores various strategies within the classroom, within the school and in the broader community and concludes that the challenge now is to formulate requirements of a 'school for all'. Anne O'Brien's article is a sensitive case study documenting the experience of one girl from a traveller family who attended a secondary school in the southeast of Ireland. In spite of the support systems set up for her, this young girl has encountered many difficulties in adjusting to life in a secondary school. The article ends with a quotation from the submission of the Association of Teachers of Travelling People to the Task Force which suggests a way forward: "In a multi-cultural society, it is essential that the education system is intercultural and anti-racist and committed to equal opportunities for everyone. For change to be effective and far-reaching, reform must be approached in a holistic way". In the third of this trilogy, Aileen O'Gorman raises a number of concerns about remedial teaching. She suggests firstly that the use of the word 'remedial teacher' should be re-examined and that consideration should be given to using 'learning support teacher' instead. She discusses questions such as the workload of the remedial teacher, his/her role within the school, the problem of isolation and the question of whole school inspection. She ends by asking whether it is realistic that the learning support teacher be expected to continue to deliver a quality service to her 'special' pupils until retirement age, given the exceptional demands of this role.

The 1937 Constitution of Ireland recognises the inalienable rights of parents in relation to the education of their children. However, it was not until the 1980s that parents were given an opportunity to be represented in education decision-making structures. The National Parents' Council has been represented on the N.C.C.A. for the past decade and has played an important part in ensuring that parent views in relation to curriculum are taken into account. The article by Pat Sexton discusses the Junior Cycle curriculum from a parent's perspective and raises some questions about approaches to assessment as well as about aspects of various subject syllabi.

Ireland is not alone in reviewing and revising its junior cycle curriculum in recent decades. Many other European countries have carried out a similar review. France is one of the countries which has been involved in educational reform and the article by Imelda Bonel-Elliott provides an overview of this reform. Under the terms of the 1996 reform in France, the junior cycle is divided into three sub-cycles: the cycle of adaptation (first year); the central cycle (second and third years) and the orientation cycle (fourth year). Instead of providing a uniform type of education, stress is now laid on adapting the curriculum to suit the local situation and on responding to the needs, aptitudes and interests of a diverse school population.

It was not possible within the confines of one volume to include an article on all subjects of the junior cycle programme. However, a number of articles in this collection provide a discussion and critique of individual subject areas. Tom Mullins gives an overview of the evolution of English at junior cycle and points out that the new syllabus introduced in 1989 challenged what he calls the "monolithic, hegemonic view of the subject" on a number of fronts. The idea of literary experience was broadened and not seen as confined exclusively to certain texts defined by their criteria; adolescent literature was given a significant role and the media found a place. While this article acknowledges the improvements that have occurred in the junior certificate examination papers, it suggests that there is an anomaly in having an open syllabus assessed only by a terminal written examination. The article by Joe Coy also raises questions about the assessment of the English syllabus. He discusses issues relating to language, literature and literacy and states that for many teachers the new syllabus is a great liberation. The appropriateness of the examination is questioned and the viewpoint is expressed that "the greatest obstacle to teaching the Junior Cert course is the Junior Cert exam". The writer asserts that modes of assessment determine to a great extent what is studied and suggests that "ingenuity, imagination and greater resources are required" if the problem of the examination is to be solved.

The new history syllabus is critiqued in some detail in an article by James O'Donoghue where he explores the theoretical foundations of the new syllabus and evaluates its reality for pupils. He points out that the breadth of the syllabus can be off-putting and confusing for teachers. However, if teachers have a clear understanding of the aims of the syllabus they may find it less daunting to select appropriate content and periods of study. Time pressures have proved to be a real problem for many teachers to date. But O'Donoghue concludes that "the new course has helped to revive junior level history" and that "students are realising the vitality, the relevance and the importance of history for them". Kenneth Milne also addresses issues relating to the teaching of history on the island of Ireland, both north and south. He recognises the inherent difficulties in teaching history in an unbiased way in a country such as ours where the folk-memory can often be "faulty and selective". But he argues that the difficulties we face in this regard should not be naively glossed over, for "it is not easy to commend one tradition to another in a political situation at the centre of which is the question of who is to exercise power". He argues that the role of the history teacher is to help pupils to develop the skills of the historian and while he recognises that this is no easy task, he maintains that "such an approach will help to familiarise pupils with the need to find out what lies behind the statements in the text book and, with experience, begin to form judgements for themselves".

The issue of foreign language teaching is discussed in an article by Catherine Fitzpatrick. She analyses the aims of the current syllabi in the context of the general aims of the Junior Certificate and of the specific aims of modern language teaching as outlined in the Report of the Board of Studies for Languages 1987. Drawing on the work of Mary Ruane in 1990, she examines three important variables which determine participation rates in the various language areas:- provision, allocation and choice. While recognising that the introduction of the Junior Cert. has resulted in many positive developments in language teaching, she argues that there are further issues which need to be addressed such as equality of access for all pupils to a modern language, diversification and increased participation rates. These issues, she believes, are unlikely to be addressed in the absence of a national policy on languages and she suggests that now is the time to formulate such a policy.

Tá alt suimiúil ag Mícheál O Brádaigh ar an Ghaeilge sa Teastas Sóisearach. Cuireann sé i gcuimhne dúinn go bhfuil an cúrsa nua ina ochtú bliain anois agus gur am tráthúil é seo chun iniúchadh a dhéanamh air. Iniúchann sé an siollabas faoi na cinnteidil seo leanas: labhairt na teanga, cluasthuiscint, léitheoireacht agus scríbhneoireacht. Déanann sé tagairt do topaicí agus feidhmeanna, do feasacht teanga agus do cultúir. Ag deiridh an ailt, deir O Brádaigh gur: "tuar dóchais is ea na hathruithe atá ag teacht i bhfeidhm i gcuraclam na bunscoile maidir leis an nGaeilge" ach ag an am gcéanna "go bhfuil gá fós le fóram a bheith ann inar féidir le múinteoirí de gach leibhéal teacht le chéile chun pleanáil a dhéanamh agus leanúnachas a chothú agus a chinntiú i dteagasc na Gaeilge".

The Minister for Education, Niamh Bhreathnach, recently announced that a new subject - Civic, Social and Political Education - will be compulsory at Junior Cycle level in all schools from September 1997. This subject will replace the old Civics programme and already almost half of the schools are offering CSPE. Michael Stokes' article chronicles the background to this development and discusses the syllabus, including teaching materials and methodology. He identifies a number of challenges facing schools in introducing this subject including timetabling, teacher education, approaches to assessment and lack of continuity to senior cycle. However, in view of what he regards as the "remarkable transformation" of Irish society, he concludes that the introduction of the new course is both timely and necessary.

Denis O'Boyle raises some interesting questions in his article on Physical Education in the junior cycle. He points out that the provision for P.E. in Irish schools is among the worst in Europe, and that Ireland is the only country which does not have compulsory P.E. at second level. He argues that P.E. is at a critical stage in its development at all levels of education but expresses some optimism that the issue can be addressed and hopefully improved. He reproduces figures from a national survey which show that whereas 80% of schools provide for two periods a week or more for First Year pupils, this falls to 42% of schools for pupils in sixth year. He highlights the lack of facilities for the teaching of P.E. and the relative shortage of P.E. teachers in Ireland compared to other countries. He addresses the issue of certification of P.E. at junior cycle and sets out the arguments for and against certification. He concludes by asserting that "the time to seriously address these issues has well and truly arrived".

The issue of Information Technology in our schools is considered in an article by John Mulcahy. This article takes as its starting point a review of I.T. in Irish schools conducted by NITEC/DCU for the European Commission in 1992. This report was critical of the absence of coherent Departmental policy for the development of IT in schools and of the lack of uniformity of IT hardware and software which makes it difficult to provide an accurate account of the level and type of activity taking place in schools. The article discusses the integration of IT into the curriculum and identifies some of its implications for teachers and classroom practice. It concludes that "the integration of IT in the curriculum is achievable if a genuine commitment exists at Government level ensuring that as we approach the end of the millennium, every school leaver is computer literate".

The final article discusses the Junior Certificate Elementary Programme - "one of the latest innovations in the Irish education system" - the aim of which is to provide an alternative approach to the junior cycle programme, specifically aimed at those young people who show signs of school failure or early leaving. In this article Aideen Cassidy points out that every year over 3,000 pupils leave school before the Junior Cert. and a further 2,400 fail to get at least five passes in that examination. The experience of school is one of failure and alienation for many of these students. The Junior Cert. Elementary Programme is designed to ensure that these young people can benefit from their time in school through acknowledging and rewarding their achievements. The article discusses the approach taken by this innovative programme and focuses on some key elements including content and teaching strategies, assessment approaches, teacher in-service and whole school support. The article concludes by looking to the future and by stating that if school authorities embrace this opportunity and actively support the intervention (i.e. JCEP) "then we in the education community can proudly say that we are striving to fulfil our obligation; to cherish all the children of the state equally".

The articles in this journal paint a positive picture of junior cycle education in Ireland. Most contributors appear to be of the opinion that changes in the curriculum in recent years have improved the quality of learning in the junior cycle classroom. That is not to say that there is overall satisfaction with the status quo nor that there is no room for improvement particularly in the area of congruence of curriculum and assessment. While there is a recognition that in many areas of school life, teachers meet considerable challenges on a day to day basis, the articles reflect the commitment of teachers to young people and a high level of professionalism in their delivery of an educational service. Ireland has good reason to be proud of its educational system as it moves into the twenty-first century.

The Introduction of the Junior Certificate: An Overview

PÁDRAIG BREATHNACH

The Junior Certificate programme was launched in 1989 for first examination in 1992. It was the result of work which was initiated in 1984, and which continues. This paper outlines the development of the programme, and focuses on some issues that merit the attention of the education community.

Background

One can not examine the introduction of the Junior Certificate in isolation from its historical context. The arrangements for second-level education in Ireland emerged on a piecemeal basis. By the 1960s a dual system was well established. Secondary schools were heavily academic; vocational schools emphasised practical studies. There were separate examination systems for each type of school. The examination taken by secondary school students at about the age of fifteen was the Intermediate Certificate. Some subjects were compulsory – Irish, English, Mathematics, History & Geography – and students normally took about four optional subjects. Vocational school students sat for the Day Vocational Certificate, commonly referred to as the Group Certificate. To qualify for certification, they had to pass a combination of subjects that was seen as having some vocational coherence. The boundaries between the two types of school and the two examining systems were strong, and there was a regrettable perception that the academic tradition of the secondary schools was somehow superior.

In the 1960s the dual system came to be seen as unsuited to the state's needs. The idea of a comprehensive curriculum was adopted. New syllabuses were developed, and existing syllabuses were revised. At the same time, the level of participation in post-primary level education was increasing, greatly assisted by the introduction of free post-primary education. Both certification schemes were maintained, and the perception of the Intermediate Certificate as the superior qualification persisted. Vocational schools moved far more towards the academic tradition than did the secondary schools move towards practical subjects.

By the 1980s – indeed long before – many believed that the comprehensivisation of the curriculum should be completed by adopting a suitable programme for all students, with a unified system for assessment and certification. This challenge was taken up by Ms. Gemma Hussey, Minister for Education. In 1984 she instituted the Curriculum and Examinations Board (CEB) and charged it with this, among other tasks.[1]

The Agencies for Change
The history of the CEB and its successor agency, the National Council for Curriculum and Assessment (NCCA), is a complex study of the politics of educational reform. It cannot be dealt with it in the scope of a brief paper. Yet the development of the Junior Cert. cannot be explained without recognising the problems which beset the key agency (the CEB and NCCA should be seen as a continuum). These included

- When the Fine Gael-led coalition of which Ms. Hussey was a member was replaced by a Fianna Fáil-led government in 1987, the future existence of the CEB became doubtful. The position was resolved by the creation of the NCCA, which was not given the statutory basis and relative independence that the CEB had anticipated.
- The Department of Education, in particular the Inspectorate who constitute its professional arm, had difficulties with delineating boundaries with the CEB/NCCA. This led to difficulties in co-ordinating functions, and to occasional conflict.
- Both Ms. Hussey and her successor, Ms. Mary O'Rourke, believed that school-based assessment (SBA) for the purposes of certification was desirable. This view was shared by many other interests, but was resisted strongly by teachers, particularly ASTI. Conflict over this matter absorbed a great deal of time and attention that might more profitably have been applied elsewhere.
- The CEB and NCCA were significantly under-resourced. The permanent executive comprised fewer than ten members, including clerical and

administrative staff. Education Officers were seconded on a short-term or part-time basis to assist in particular tasks. Most decision-making was formally the business of the Board or Council, who operated through the executive and through a network of committees. Committee members commonly complained that there were not enough meetings to allow full consideration of important matters, and that executive service, although generally of high quality, was insufficient.

- The Board and the Council had also to deal with other issues, including a review of the primary curriculum, the development of Transition Year and the initiation of a revision of senior cycle provision.

In spite of these and other difficulties, the amount of work undertaken was impressive. The development and launch of the Junior Cert. programme in just over five years was an outstanding achievement attained in adverse conditions.

Delivery of product is one thing. The important question to ask is if it was worth the wait. This is the question which is addressed in this paper.

THE AIMS OF THE JC PROGRAMME
Assumptions about Junior Cycle
Two factors affected the view taken of curriculum in the junior cycle

- Existing programmes had been drawn up on the basis that second-level education was an option exercised by a minority. The corollary was that any essential educational experience needed to be delivered in primary education. The raising of the school-leaving age to fifteen, and an increased participation in post-compulsory education had changed that.
- There was an unstated assumption that the needs of the individual in modern society were greater than in the past, and that the essential educational experience needed to be extended.

Curriculum Principles
The CEB proposed a number of principles which should underpin curriculum structure. They included **breadth & balance** and **relevance** to the needs of young people.[2] These were not contested, and have been echoed in all important statements since. There were other proposals that implied recognition of the varying circumstances, abilities and needs of students: flexibility, differentiation and adaptability. These were not picked up so

readily, and are not foregrounded in NCCA or Department of Education documents on junior cycle. Instead, there is an emphasis on **quality** of student achievement "having regard to their different aptitudes and abilities".[3]

Curriculum Structure

In 1984 the CEB issued, for consultation, a framework of eight 'categories' which all students should experience. Core elements and additional contributions were suggested for each category. Considerable effort was made to link this model with existing subject areas. Some new subject possibilities also emerged, such as Social & Political Education, New Technologies, and Consumer Education.[4] This model was heavily influenced by – some would say derived from – work conducted in Scotland in the late 1970s.[5] In response to submissions (which included some vigorous campaigning) a modified structure was developed and recommended to the Minister for Education (Mr. Patrick Cooney) in March 1986. The areas of experience proposed were:

- Arts education
- Guidance & Counselling
- Languages & Literature (a. Vernacular; b. Other)
- Mathematical Studies
- Physical Education
- Religious Education
- Science & Technology
- Social, Political & Environmental Studies.[6]

These recommendations were not expressly accepted or rejected. Shortly afterwards the government fell and, in consequence, the CEB was abolished and replaced by the NCCA. In that process, the proposals for curriculum structure fell into abeyance.

The NCCA attempted to maintain the model. A *Green Paper* on Education was proposed by Minister O'Rourke. Her successors, Mr. Noel Davern, and Mr. Seamus Brennan, each sought revisions before it was issued in 1992. It became clear to the NCCA that its proposed curriculum structure might not be favoured.[7] A more modest proposal was made for the short or medium term that the compulsory core of full subjects be: Irish; English; Mathematics; Science; History/Geography or Environmental & Social Studies[8]. The possibility of substituting a technological subject for Science was acknowledged.

An elaborate consultative process was conducted following the publication of the *Green Paper,* including holding a National Education Convention during 1993. This contributed to the development of the *White Paper on Education* published in 1995. The proposals for compulsory subjects set out there were: Irish, English, Mathematics, a science or a technological subject, and at least three further subjects.[9] There was no mention of History or Geography being compulsory, although they had been so in secondary schools since the foundation of the state. During 1996 concern was expressed that a new programme in Civic, Social & Political Education might supplant History & Geography. This led to intensive lobbying by interest groups, and Minister for Education Niamh Bhreathnach referred the question to the NCCA in terms which suggested that they should accede to the demands for the retention of History and Geography as core subjects.[10]

Elements of Learning & Syllabus Development

In 1986 the CEB identified 'elements of learning'. They were stated to be knowledge, concepts, skills and attitudes.[11] This model was appropriated from a discussion paper circulated in the UK.[12] It is regrettable that the model was not subjected to critical analysis before being proposed here, and remarkable that it was later quietly dropped.

Course Committees were convened to undertake syllabus development. Their function was broadly analogous to that of the Syllabus Committees that had functioned previously but with the following enhancements to their brief:

- to devise unified syllabuses (to replace Inter Cert. and Group Cert. syllabuses) which might be examined at two or three levels;
- to state assessment objectives and develop examining guidelines;
- to produce guidelines for teachers;
- to draw up syllabuses that were based on the elements of learning.

The first task – devising unified syllabuses – had been required by Minister Hussey. The next two, which extended the role of the committees, could be seen as useful work. It was the brief to adopt a particular model of learning which was most interesting. It might have contributed to problems in planning assessment schemes.

The committees accepted their remits, and syllabuses were developed. Most of them reflected the 'elements of learning' model. In doing this, they displayed great resourcefulness, as they were not offered any substantial explanations of the elements. As the work progressed, the NCCA went in a different direction, virtually subverting the committees' brief. It dropped the model, and substituted a fresh list: knowledge, understanding, skills and competencies.[13]

Implementation
The simple thing to say about implementation of the new programme in 1989 is that is was successful. Ten new or revised syllabuses were prescribed, teachers were given guidelines and training, and public awareness initiatives were undertaken as preparation for introducing the programme. In the following years, further syllabuses were introduced. The first Junior Cert. examination was held in 1992. In the small number of years since, it has become firmly established both among the education community and in the public eye and it is widely accepted and respected.

Assessment
The Junior Cert. combines a curriculum and a certification scheme. For the purposes of certification, a student's achievement of programme aims needs to the measured. Assessment is an important dimension of the Junior Cert; it might be remembered that the primary objective was the unification of two separate certification schemes.

School-Based Assessment
The contested issue in Junior Cert. was SBA. The idea was flagged from the very beginning, in the CEB's terms of reference. The Board accepted the suggestion, and recommended its introduction.[14] Teacher interests, particularly the ASTI, resisted strongly. The Board and, in succession, the Council continued to advocate it. When the Junior Cert. programme was introduced in 1989 teacher interests believed that they had prevailed. They were surprised and greatly angered when in September 1990 Minister O'Rourke revived the proposal.[15] The Council responded very positively to the Minister's suggestion, and this led to sharp exchanges between the ASTI, the

NCCA and the Minister. The matter was largely resolved when the Council was reconstituted in January 1991, and the question of SBA was sidelined.

Validity

All sides might have chosen the wrong battlefield. The crucial issues in assessment are not where or when it is conducted, or by whom it is administered or scored. The important matters are *validity* (that a test measures what it is supposed to measure) and *reliability* (that it does so with a reasonable degree of precision). Clearly validity precedes reliability: precise measurement is meaningless if what is being measured is not properly defined. SBA is a reliability issue, and is not a real issue until the question of validity has been determined. This is where, despite its general acceptance, the Junior Certificate is most deficient. No steps were ever taken to assure validity. Validity assurance is a complex technical operation that is beyond the scope of this paper. It is, regrettably, a question to which little attention is paid in Ireland.

Validity revolves around the idea of a **construct.** In assessment terms, a construct is the set of behaviours that indicate mastery of a subject. It is somewhat artificial: school French is not the same as all French. Constructs demarcate subjects. The constructs of History and Music should be distinguishable from one another. At a surface level, they certainly appear to be: 'doing' History does not seem the same as 'doing' music. Similarly, skills in English differ from skills in Science.

For a test in a particular subject to be valid, there must be a discernible difference between performance in that subject and performance in other subjects. A test in Irish aims to measure something different from a test in Art, Craft & Design. Test items, including examination questions, are not always properly targeted. A candidate who reproduces, without comprehension, a definition in a Business Studies test and another definition in a Geography test might not be proving significant capacity or achievement in either subject. On the other hand, a candidate who deals well with a comprehension item in a History test might be given credit in History for what is essentially performance in English.

The NCCA and the course committees treated constructs as pre-existing, and to be taken for granted. At the same time, they were engaged in attempts to redefine subjects to accord with the elements of learning model. In general, they seem not to have attended to the tension between the two positions. They were also tasked with designing assessment schemes without having recourse to assessment expertise other than some degree of familiarity with existing examining practices. These had been devised for different types of syllabus and had already come under criticism.[16] The extreme case of difficulty in addressing constructs was that of Technology. This was introduced as a new subject in 1989, and this writer was a member of the committee that drew up the syllabus. He can testify that the surest way to discommode the committee was to ask the question: "what is Technology?" Yet if one cannot answer the question, how can one devise a course, determine objectives, and draw up a scheme of assessment? One wonders if course committees dealing with Irish or Geography or Business Studies were at all troubled by such issues.

Conclusions

The Junior Cert. was introduced principally as a mechanism for unifying two assessment and certification systems. In undertaking this the CEB and NCCA attempted to

- develop a rational curriculum structure;
- improve the quality of syllabus development;
- ensure better communication of syllabus intention;
- make assessment follow rather than lead syllabus; and
- broaden the basis of assessment.

The unification of certification systems was very successfully achieved. Progress in the other areas was limited. There were a number of reasons for this:

- failures in planning;
- successful opposition;
- a lack of support for innovation.

1   Ms. Gemma Hussey, TD, Minister for Education, "Curriculum and Examinations Board: Terms of Reference," Specific term 1.
2   Curriculum & Examinations Board *In Our Schools: A Framework for Curriculum and Assessment* (Dublin: CEB, 1986) pp. 14-15.

3   Ireland (Department of Education) *Charting Our Education Future: White Paper on Education* (Dublin: Stationery Office, 1995) p. 47.

4   Curriculum & Examinations Board *Issues and Structures in Education: A Consultative Document* (Dublin: CEB, 1984) pp. 16-20.

5   United Kingdom (Scottish Office) *Munn Report: The Structure of the Curriculum in the Third and Fourth Years of the Scottish Secondary School* (London: HMSO, 1977).

6   CEB, *In Our Schools* pp.19-21.

7   Ireland (Department of Education) *Education for a Changing World: Green Paper on Education* (Dublin: Stationery Office, 1992) pp. 93-95.

8   National Council for Curriculum & Assessment, *Programme for Reform: Curriculum and Assessment Policy Towards the New Century* (Dublin: NCCA, 1993) p.33.

9   Dept. of Education, *White Paper,* p. 49.

10 History and Geography were not core subjects in all schools; only in secondary schools. On the same date that she instructed the NCCA, Minister Breathnach assured Dáil Éireann that the subjects were not under threat.

11 The 'elements of learning' were first stated in *"In Our Schools"* p. 22.

12 United Kingdom (Department of Education and Science) *The Curriculum from 5 to 16 (Curriculum Matters 2: An HMI Series)* (London: HMSO. 1985) pp. 36-42.

13 National Council for Curriculum and Assessment, *Guide to the Junior Cert.* (Dublin: NCCA, 1989) p. 13. This listing emerged after course committees had completed all or most of their work. Nonetheless, it appears in the standard preamble to all syllabus documents.

14 Curriculum and Examinations Board, *Assessment and Certification: A Consultative Document* (Dublin: CEB, 1985) p.11.

15 She did so formally in a letter to the NCCA's Chief Executive dated 18 September 1990.

16 See Curriculum and Examinations Board *Assessment and Certification: A Consultative Document* (Dublin: CEB, 1985) pp. 6-7

БИБЛ

TEACHER DEVELOPMENT WITH PARTICULAR REFERENCE TO JUNIOR CYCLE CHANGE

DAVID TUOHY

The influx of a large number of students into Irish secondary schools in the 1970's provided a major challenge to the system, particularly to the curriculum. It was easy to blame the student for failing in the existing system, rather than to examine the system in which the student was failing. Since then, however, major changes in curriculum have taken place, and the Junior Certificate is an example of this development. As well as being a response to practical classroom experience, the new curriculum reflects major philosophical shifts in the understanding of knowledge itself, on the nature of truth and value, on how learning takes place, and on the nature of intelligence. These can be represented as a series of bi-polar tensions (Brooks and Brooks, 1993):

Traditional	Modern
Curriculum is presented part to whole, with emphasis on basic skills	Curriculum is presented whole to part, with emphasis on big concepts
Strict adherence to fixed curriculum is highly valued	Pursuit of student questions is highly valued
Curricular activities rely heavily on textbooks and workbooks	Curricular activities rely heavily on primary sources of data and manipulative materials
Students are viewed as "blank slates" onto which information is etched by the teacher	Students are viewed as thinkers with emerging theories about the world
Teachers generally behave in a didactic manner, disseminating information to students	Teachers generally behave in an interactive manner, mediating the environment for students

Traditional	Modern
Teachers seek the correct answer to validate student learning	Teachers seek the students' points of view in order to understand students' present conceptions for use in subsequent lessons
Assessment of student learning is viewed as separate from teaching and occurs almost entirely through testing	Assessment of student learning is interwoven with teaching and occurs through teacher observations of students at work and through student exhibitions and portfolios
Students primarily work alone	Students primarily work in groups

As many teachers have been trained to cope with the older approach to curriculum, the introduction of the Junior Certificate had implications for rethinking the in-service of teachers. This article reflects on the models of in-service which might contribute to the further development of the Junior Cycle.

The Aims of In-Service

The change process involved in the Junior Cycle must capture both the mind and the heart of the teacher. It is not simply a change in content, nor it is a matter of developing slightly new tricks. Central to the new curriculum is a different attitude to knowledge, learning and the student. It involves reconceptualising the role of the teacher, and the teacher's relationship with the student. The in-service required for the success of the Junior Cycle requires that the elements of teacher knowledge and skills is addressed, but also that teachers be given a chance to develop new attitudes to their role.

Glickman (1981) has proposed a model of teacher development which looks at these two dimensions. Knowledge and skills are considered as the technical and practical aspects of teaching - understanding what is to be taught and have the pedagogical skills to facilitate learning by the student. Teachers can be rated LOW or HIGH on these skills. Attitudes refer to the affective side of teaching - the teacher's sense of commitment, enthusiasm, belief in what he or she is doing, motivation, etc. Again, a teacher can be rated as LOW or HIGH in this area. When combined, this gives rise to four types of teacher:

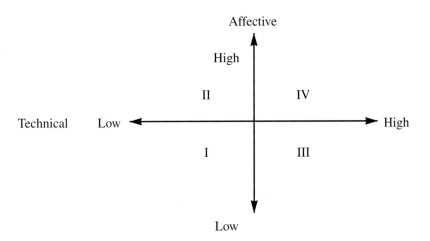

Quadrant I refers to teachers who are low on both technical and affective skills. They do not believe in the changes proposed, and they do not have the necessary skills to implement the course. At an extreme, such teachers may be considered as dropouts or burnouts. They no longer practise the skills they once had, and they no longer have a taste for teaching.

Quadrant II refers to teachers who have great enthusiasm for the new curriculum, but they are weak on the technical skills required for teaching it. Such teachers are sometimes named as Zealots. Frequently these teachers move from one project to another, initiating them with great enthusiasm, but leaving it to others to maintain and complete them. They talk eloquently about the purpose of the Junior Cycle, but the classroom results fail to match the rhetoric.

Quadrant III refers to teachers who are highly competent in the classroom, but somehow disengaged from the purpose of the new curriculum. They may have developed their expertise in the old curriculum, and now pass as Observers on the new curriculum. At an extreme, they are cynical about others around them, and offer an incisive but destructive commentary on their efforts, with no commitment to helping the improvement process.

Quadrant IV refers to the Professional teacher who is highly competent and committed. These teachers adapt their skills to the changing demands of different programmes and students. They face change in a genuinely critical way, measuring proposals against their own vision of education and the evidence of developing theory and practice.

The aim of teacher development is to move to the professional quadrant. Each of the quadrants represents different types of teachers, and the needs and growth of each will be different. In-service training which aims to spray-paint all teachers so that everyone looks the same, thinks the same and teaches the same way, is doomed to failure. The need in the training process is to understand what it is that moves people along each of the axes - the technical and the affective. But we also need to know what moves people backwards, why people regress into non-productive world views which stifle their growth and creativity. We also need to know what keeps them there. The answer does not always lie within the individual teacher. Frequently, the causes lie in non-supportive structures within the school itself, a lack of resources or inappropriate assessment procedures related to the aims of the curriculum. Addressing these issues is a central aspect of the in-service programme.

Issues of Development

1. Extra-personal challenge The extra-personal skills of teachers refer to the technical aspects of knowledge of subject matter and pedagogical skills. Changing approaches to knowledge and learning have been outlined at the beginning of the article. There is a tension between the old approach and the new approach. The requirement for teachers is a balance between a totally deductive and a totally inductive approach. The danger is that teachers fail to live with the tension, and they opt for one approach over the other. Thus, there grows up two types of teacher, dividing the staffroom into

- the "soft" teachers who give great process through projects and discussions, but who are weak on challenge and content and
- the "real" teachers who grind out the points for success, but whose classes are controlled, predictable, repetitious and dull.

The aim of in-service in extra-personal skills is not to see the two skill set as "either/or", but rather as "both/and". Thus, each teacher has a wide range of skills to draw from and can use the appropriate skill in a particular situation. The alternative can be illustrated by the old saying - "If the only skill you have is hammering, then you tend to see every problem as a nail". The variety of skills ensures a professional response to the wider variety of challenges which a teacher must face in promoting learning.

2. Inter-personal challenge. Traditionally, teacher leadership and authority has sought compliant responses from students. This has determined a style of relating to students. However, the new curriculum requires skills of students which are far from compliant, and this makes new demands on the type of relationship between student and teacher.

A large number of students come from disadvantaged backgrounds, where their academic experience or ambition may not have been nurtured. Often, teachers have little understanding of the stress in the lives of such students. An adequate response requires that pastoral care become an integral part of all subjects and all classroom work, rather than an optional function somewhere in the curriculum. This also requires new student-teacher relationships.

The large number of older students in our schools have personal experiences of travel, work, relationships and independence outside the school which mean that they are less likely to accept a compliant role within the school. This poses a challenge to traditional concepts of discipline, and there is a need to explore new structures of relationships and model more democratic ways of involving students in their own learning.

Teachers must also develop relationships which are appropriate to the age gap between themselves and their students. It is readily recognised that grandparents have a different nurturing role to parents, and this in turn differs from the big brother or sister relationship with a younger sibling. As teachers gain in "chronological advantage", they experience and accept these changed relationships in their personal lives, but frequently fail to apply them to their professional relationships and expectations of students. Finding the balance is an important part of teacher interpersonal development, and is a legitimate part of teacher inservice.

3. Intra-Personal Challenge The intra-personal aspect of teaching refers to the sense of identity that teachers have, the metaphors they have for their own work, their sense of mission and purpose. This can be challenged both from the internal dynamics of the school, and also from external pressures.

The constant pressures for change can be very wearying on teachers. This pressure is reminiscent of the two Arabs wandering in the desert. It is a natural question to keep on asking "Are we nearly there"?, but in truth, they never arrive at a destination, because they are in fact nomads. When this image is applied to teachers, it is natural to yearn for being settlers - where life is more controlled, more predictable. The challenge that exists is the reconceptualisation of the profession to take into account the changing demands of teaching and relationships. Teachers perhaps need to redefine themselves as nomads, constantly moving in the desert of change. In taking on this new role, the desert is no longer seen as a threat, and the individual can grasp and enjoy this new role. The change process up to now has been burdensome. The lack of prioritisation had meant that teachers have taken on more and more roles and burdens, and shed none of the older ones. The catch phrase must now become: "Teachers will work smarter, not harder".

This means some radical redefinition of the appropriate function and role of the teachers rather than constantly accepting new and added responsibilities. But this redefinition must take place in a spirit of dialogue and trust, in an atmosphere which seeks to cater for the needs of the system, not just the security of the teacher. (Tuohy and Coghlan, 1994).

The current identity of the profession reflects the history of Irish education, and it also defines the capacity of the system to change and develop. It is essential that this area of identity be addressed, and that the dynamic and ever-evolving professional identity of teachers inform curricular developments and responses to the other challenges facing the teacher. A major question arises as to where the leadership for this new identity will be found. It may well be found within the teaching profession itself, where some one leader or group will encourage teachers to reflect on and take a proactive role in their emerging identity. However, there is also a danger that teachers will fail to find a common identity, and that some outside authority will impose an identity that will ultimately turn teachers into technicians in their own service. The key to successful development is a dialogue between the stakeholders in education.

Approaches to Training
The approach to in-service training can work from three main models:

1. Remedial Approach, in which a diagnosis is made of what is lacking in the teacher, and a training programme is set up to remove the deficiencies.

Frequently, the teacher is coerced into participation in the service.

2. Cultural Approach, in which information about courses, journals, etc. are available, but it is left up to the individual to look after his/her own development. The environment provides the opportunity, but the responsibility for consumption and growth is the individuals.

3. A Comprehensive Approach takes place when a programme of development is worked out to take account of the personal needs of the individual teachers and also the organisational needs of the system. (Tuohy, 1995).

Initial teacher training has mixed the remedial and the cultural. On a theory level, the student is provided with a cultural feast in lectures, in the hope that they are hungry enough to eat. The approach to teaching practice on the other hand has often been to correct faults and to develop strategies which eliminate classroom problems.

Until recently, the main approach to in-service has been cultural, with "refresher" courses taking place in holiday time, when it has been hoped that teachers would avail of the limited menu on offer - and that menu mainly focused on the extrapersonal skills area of development. When this approach was diagnosed as being inadequate, a more remedial and coercive approach was advocated by requiring teachers to attend one day in-service courses, and this has more sinister implications in a demand for general "evaluation" and "remediation" systems for teachers.

What is called for is a shift to a comprehensive approach, in which a dialogue is opened with the teachers where their real needs are heard and responded to, and the needs of the system are shared with them. We can discern the beginnings of such a shift when we contrast the model of inservice offered at the introduction of the Junior Cycle, and the inservice provided for the Transition Year and for the current LCAP. These latter approaches aim to meet the needs of teachers in their own situation, and to offer some support and help rather than imposing direction on them. There is a need to continue and develop this comprehensive and consultative approach.

These reflections give rise to three main implications for in-service.

1. Time for reflection and planning. There is a need to build into the definition of the profession the structures of reflective practice. This requires that time be given to reflection and planning. No one would seriously propose trying to service their car while they were driving at 60 miles per hour down the Naas Dual carriageway. However, the present practice of inservice often seems to ask the equivalent of teachers.

2. Balance between the personal and professional development of the teacher. The current focus of inservice is very much focused on extra-personal skills. However, this needs to be balanced with the personal development needs of teachers. As Bryan McMahon says in his autobiography, a good teacher is a good person who teaches. Investment in the personal development of the teacher will undoubtedly have benefits in their professional development as well.

3. Beyond pedagogical competence. The focus of school and teacher development must go beyond "schooling" and focus on education. Schooling takes place where society invests resources in particular learning experiences. However, people learn in other places besides school. They learn from their families, their friends, their local communities, from developing technologies. If teachers are to move beyond competence to excellence, then the profession must forge new partnerships with all those other providers of education. These include partnerships with primary teachers, parents and the world of work. Particularly, teachers must also understand the way in which the future is being shaped for their students, and constructively contribute to that future. It would be a shame if teachers were to develop their expertise in preparing students for the world, only to find that their particular version of the world no longer existed (Bales, 1996). Perhaps the key to this development is that teachers have less focus on teaching as such, and focus instead on learning - that they define themselves as experts in the learning process. When learning becomes the focus of reflection, then perhaps the curriculum and in-service needs take on new perspectives and new possibilities. It is then that teachers will begin to shape their own profession and take their respected place in shaping the future for students.

Bales, E. (1996) In an interview with Denis Sparkes, National Staff Development Council tape.

Brooks, J.G. and Brooks, M.G. (1993) *In Search of Understanding. The Case for Constructivist Classrooms.* Washington, D.C.: Association for Supervision and Curriculum Development.

Glickman, C.D. (1981) *Development Supervision: Alternative Practices for Helping Teachers Improve Instruction.* Washington, D.C.: Association for Supervision and Curriculum Development.

Tuohy, D. (1995) Teacher Self-Evaluation. Discipline or Dyslexia in the Learning Organisation. *Irish Educational Studies.* Vol. 14 pp. 64-82.

Tuohy, D. and Coghlan, D. (1994) Integrating Teacher and School Development through Organisational Levels. *Oideas* Vol. 42 pp. 83-97.

ACTIVE LEARNING IN THE CLASSROOM: A CHALLENGE TO EXISTING EDUCATIONAL VALUES AND PRACTICES.

JIM CALLAN

Why Active Learning?:
There are various reasons why active learning in the classroom is encouraged. Active learning, it is suggested, provides opportunities for involving pupils in what is going on and so it helps gain their attention, it helps to motivate them in their learning. Moreover, having active forms of learning enables the teacher to address a wider range of learning styles among pupils: some pupils can learn through book work while some pupils learn better through engaging in such activities as project work, fieldwork, role play.

A further reason why one would advocate active learning in the classroom is because it is a necessary requirement for **understanding a subject.** To study a subject is to *participate* in that subject. Specifically, how to *engage* in its form of inquiry, how to *apply* the knowledge, how to *use* the language of the subject, how to *think* in the subject. This challenges us to critically review the kind of knowledge we have traditionally valued in our schools.

Active Learning and the Junior Certificate:
It is precisely this challenge which the introduction of the Junior Certificate has presented to our schools. In the literature accompanying the Junior Certificate, viz. Guidelines for Teachers, an emphasis is placed on imparting the skills of inquiry associated with the subject discipline. For example:

...the method of teaching must allow the student to learn through active participation in both practical and experimental work... There should be an emphasis on the thought processes of science as well as the knowledge content. **(Science: Guidelines for Teachers)** [the course] must provide opportunity for genuine discovery and problem-solving thus developing skills of the geographer.

(Geography: Guidelines for Teachers)

in… the English course [students] should be encouraged to use, explore, develop, refine the language that is most immediate and closest to themselves. **(English: Guidelines for Teachers)**

one of the special features of this course is the way in which it emphasises the methods of historical enquiry as well as the content of history.

(History: Guidelines for Teachers)

These indicate the intention to have pupils ***participate*** in the subject in the sense I have already referred to. There are significant implications here for the role of the teacher in the teaching-learning interactions in the classroom. In addition, there are implications for how we organise our learning formats in the school and how we resource these. There are, most importantly, serious questions to be asked about the *kind of knowledge* schools ought to be imparting.

Traditionally our schools have valued *content* knowledge. This has informed our organisation of learning formats into 35/40 minute class periods. It has also informed the approach to pupil learning through the use of *textbook* material, and our emphasis on the *transmission* of knowledge. Our standards for judging what is worthwhile learning in this traditional teaching-learning situation are based on values which are significantly different from the values which inform the perspectives of the syllabus writers of the Junior Certificate programme. In the case of English essay writing, for example, prior to the Junior Certificate programme primacy was given to the acquisition of formal characteristics of writing: grammar, sentence structure, extensive vocabulary, and range of punctuation, achievements not easily won and achievements still to be admired. Essay writing in Junior Certificate English, however, places an emphasis on reflective writing which contains a personal quality and which affects pupils as persons: their language, their manners, their wisdom.

The difference between the Junior Certificate and previous programmes **is not a matter of technique but a matter of value-judgement,** i.e. what knowledge is judged to be of value. Previous programmes valued *conformity* while the Junior Certificate promotes a *sense of exploration;* previous programmes valued *correctness,* i.e. attention to structures and rules, while the

Junior Certificate values *creativity;* previous programmes valued *factual knowledge* while the Junior Certificate encourages *capability in problem-solving, inquiring, and experimental procedures.*

Active Learning in School: Some Issues:
Delivering a curriculum which emphasises experimental/discovery learning, and which requires access to a variety of source material both inside and outside the school, needs a different *school organisational structure* than is currently in place in our schools. Moreover, such a curriculum challenges teachers to re-examine their *role* in teaching-learning interactions.

Experience in the initiative **Schools for Active Learning,** an initiative which focused on providing supports for teachers of the Junior Certificate, has shown that issues of school organisation and teacher role were not addressed in the implementation processes for the Junior Certificate. Failure to take account of the school contexts into which the Junior Certificate was being implemented explains, in part, why active learning has not been realised to the degree intended by the syllabus writers and policy makers.

It is necessary to devote as much attention to the context into which the curriculum is to be implemented, as to the design of the product itself. One wonders if the writers of the various syllabi for the Junior Certificate programme could be characterised as people who had 'true belief' and 'crusading sentiments'. While no one would doubt their commitment one has to ask if their commitment is to non-existent structures which at best can be characterised as a commitment to abstract ideas and ideals, and at worst to poorly defined teacher roles. Put simply, there is a serious mis-match between the curriculum *intentions* of the Junior Certificate programme and the *reality* of school milieu in which they are to be realised. The reality of school-learning can be profiled with such descriptors as: *'primarily didactic in nature, the teacher is the primary initiator; students work alone; lessons are structured around content with a focus on factual content; little or no small group problem-solving approaches; little use of computers/video technology.* (cf. OECD: Review: Ireland). The academic goals which are the primary focus of schools are achieveable through didactic teaching systems. These goals, which significantly are manifest in examination papers, form and shape the roles and structures in our schools. An examination of the *goals, roles, and structures* in our system ought to have been addressed, simultaneously, with the introduction of a programme premised on different educational values than currently existed. Accordingly, a number of significant issues surround the Junior Certificate.

1. Structural Issues:

The issue of 'time':

Schools organise 'time' with reference to the requirements to cover a course for examination purposes. Forty minute subject class periods, eight subjects a day provides, it is believed, a reasonably effective way of covering a textbook treatment of a subject area. This construction of school time reflects the construction held of school knowledge viz. knowledge is something which is contained in text-books and which is transmitted at short intervals to young people. Moreover, it should be noted that textbooks have been commercially 'well-honed' with respect to the form of examination questions.

In discussions with teachers 'time' was mentioned as a critical factor which determines whether they use active learning methods in their classroom. This emerged in different ways. A timetable which is constructed around 40 minute class periods is considered inappropriate to realise such activities as project work, field study, and programmes designed to develop research skills. In addition, active learning formats which require out of school pupil work require class supervision for those teachers accompanying pupils engaged in such work. This places an additional workload on teachers who already have a heavy workload. A further problem arises when teachers have only three periods per week with a class. Teachers are reluctant to give time on active learning approaches when their concern is to cover a wide course (content) for examination purposes. Time is also a problem in relation to teacher planning time for active learning. They perceive active learning classes as requiring time to prepare materials, to garner ideas, to discuss with some colleagues ways of approaching topics. But in a crowded curriculum and a heavy teaching schedule whatever time teachers have for preparing class work primacy is given to preparing Leaving Certificate classes.

Absence of curriculum coherence:

The Leaving Certificate is *the* major concern for teachers. Tasks or activities which are irrelevant to this concern are put to one side. Active learning in Junior Certificate classes, for example, is not considered necessary for obtaining a good grasp of subject content, a basic requirement for covering the Leaving Certificate programme. Accordingly, many teachers teach the Junior Certificate syllabus with an eye to the requirements of the Leaving Certificate syllabus.

Coupled with 'time' is the issue of *curriculum coherence.* From the perspective of the Junior Certificate active learning is seen as an intrinsic part of what it means to study a subject, as well as a means for personal and social development of pupils. From the perspective of Leaving Certificate requirements, however, teachers see such methods as "games", "fancy frills" and "not dealing with the real knowledge of the subject". The two programmes, it is perceived, value different kinds of knowledge. And the knowledge favoured by teachers is that which has been socially legitimated through the examination system. Considering parental expectations and the career aspirations of pupils it is not surprising that teachers have been reluctant to move away from existing pedagogical systems. Under the circumstances, it is legitimate for teachers to ask: How does the Junior Certificate fit into what we are doing and the purposes for which we are doing it? Will it work in my class? Is this new emphasis on active learning practical and desirable given my teaching context? Little appreciation has been taken of the legitimacy of these questions or of addressing them in a professional manner.

Physical Environment:

'Order' and 'control' are features which describe a classroom setting. Large numbers of pupils require control measures; teacher-centred learning requires the silent attention of pupils. What one encounters in our schools is a desire for ordered and quiet procedures in learning. In many instances this is forced on schools because of poor working conditions: bad insulation, working in pre-fab buildings, inadequate levels of resources, and large class sizes. Noise is a factor which dampens teachers' enthusiasm for engaging in activities. Activities which generate noise can 'disrupt' the level of acceptable noise people have become accustomed to. Potential conflicts with a colleague in an adjacent class because of noise levels is deemed not worth the trouble. One also has to overcome an attitude that where there is noise, there is disorder and therefore no learning. School ethos can be a powerful constraint to engaging in active methods.

Inadequate audio-visual equipment can also militate against active learning. The inconvenience of having to bring an overhead projector, for example, from one building to another, or to have to book one a day or two in advance, can be too bothersome when a teacher has a lot of other things to do.

While these matters may appear as insignificant trivia, in real school life these elements in the workplace do influence what teachers do.

Class Profile:

By class profile I refer to class size, class behaviour, and class expectations. These factors influence the style of teaching which occurs in a classroom. Many teachers have indicated, for example, that using "group work" or "role play" in the class implies that the teacher has established "good order and control in the class". They noted that these methods require pupils to concentrate on the task, that pupils can work together for a period of time, and that they can take and execute directions. They maintain that it takes time and effort to establish the kind of rapport, discipline, and co-operation with certain pupils before such methods can be used. This can be very difficult to obtain in many classes: pupils may either lack interest in what is going on or they may find such methods irrelevant to their examination requirements as they perceive them.

These class contexts can lead to stressful teaching environments in which teachers resort to strategies of teaching which are designed for *coping* with the situation rather than for generating innovative or creative teaching. In practice this means teacher-controlled situations aimed at achieving coverage and mastery of content.

2. Teachers' Values:

Factors such as 'time', physical environment', class expectations', and different sets of values informing consecutive programme, ensure that the classroom has only a limited potential for manipulation by teachers. Teachers work in an environment which contains demands and constraints that are inherent in its nature given existing goals and structures of schools. Coping with these is made more difficult for teachers when new curriculum programmes, which entail new skills and roles for teachers, are introduced. In addition to structural constraints which teachers have to cope with the teachers' values and role has also been challenged.

For years teachers have known what has had to be done in class. In preparing their lessons they can predict with a high degree of certainty what is required in terms of classroom activities, materials to be used, time to be spent and the work required of pupils. There is a fixed and stable expectation among teachers about how and what to teach.

Adhering to known teaching approaches gives teachers a *sense of security.* As one teacher acknowledged *'everyone works out how they present their subject… and this is invariably around course coverage for the examinations'.* Finding out what 'works' is pursued in consort with the value system of the school. Teachers adjust to this system because it is the one in which they must shape their careers. It is not surprising, therefore, that teachers have been reluctant to use active methods. In so far as their practice 'works' it confers on them, with their peers and others, the status of a successful teacher. In doing so, such practices provide a secure context for them. When, therefore, it is suggested that their 'workable' classroom methods be altered, this status is threatened. Frequently this can be accompanied with a 'fear of failure' with unknown and untried teaching methods. As one teacher succinctly put it: *fear stops you using these methods not knowledge.'*

The Human Factor and Change:

What is revealed here is the human factor in change. At the micro level of curriculum change there is the *subjective* world of the teacher which embraces their anxieties and expectations. Specifically, teachers' *feelings of inadequacy* arise when they confront something different which brings them into a world of uncertainty. Teachers are uncertain about whether they can cope with new knowledge and new ways of working and relating with students.

Accordingly, there is an **allegiance to routines.** Routinised behaviour dulls one's sense of the need for change. Routines become 'sacred' and are legitimated on the basis of: 'this is what we have always done and by and large it has worked'. Another feature of the subjective world of the teacher is a *sense of alienation:* when new changes are introduced. The ordinary teacher, it is perceived, has little influence in shaping these changes. They tend to arrive in the school as an imposition from 'outside' forces and these can be perceived as 'forces of alienation': they display little sensitivity or appreciation of the existing teacher workload. New programmes are ruefully observed. The other side of this scenario is the *denial of personal responsibility.* There is a tendency for individual teachers to excuse their non-involvement in new programmes on the basis of the absence of adequate supports whether in the form of money or proper school management. There is a reluctance to apportion any responsibility towards oneself for not engaging in change proposals.

Finally, there are the **confines of teacher biography:** Traditionally our education system has not encouraged risk taking; it has fostered a conservatism which has 'canonised' the known, the secure; it has fostered traditional values which favoured adherence to a particular code of behaviour and thinking and which was intolerant of differences from that code.

Teachers themselves have been fostered in this *culture of containment.*

They do not perceive themselves as agents for cultural change. By training and by cultural circumstances they tend to address the immediate, the practical and the pragmatic features of their situation.

Conclusion:

In discussions on why the Junior Certificate has not been realised to the extent intended, in particular active learning formats, it is generally said that this is because of the examination format. It is difficult to disagree with this observation. However, to put in place an examination format that would better reflect the intentions of the Junior Certificate will require more than a technical adjustment to the existing system by way of, for example, payment to teachers for engaging in pupil assessment. This is only one issue, and in some respects not the most critical issue facing a system which seriously wishes to realise active learning in the classrooms of our schools. Much work remains to be done at both the institutional level and at the level of teacher's values. Fundamentally, there is a values shift involved in moving to active learning. This requires deeper appreciation than it has received to date.

Archer, Peter. (1994): *An External Evaluation of Schools for Active Learning,* published by the Author.

Callan, Jim (1994): *Schools for Active Learning: Final Report,* Education Department, Maynooth College.

Review of National Policies for Education: Ireland (1991), O.E.C.D., Paris.

The Junior Certificate: Guidelines for Teachers: The National Council for Curriculum and Assessment/ An Roinn Oideachais.

Unfreezing the Frame: Implications of Multiple Intelligences Theory for Curriculum and Assessment

Joan Hanafin

the final word on intelligence has not yet been spoken[1]

Changing constructs of intelligence

In the latter part of the twentieth century, constructs of intelligence have become more complex. There has been an indisputable move away from understanding intelligence as a unitary capacity, measurable by an IQ test. Three theories which take a systems[2] approach to understanding the nature of intelligence have been proposed in the last 15 years: Robert Sternberg's triarchic theory of human intelligence, Howard Gardner's theory of Multiple Intelligences (MI) and Stephen Ceci's bioecological treatise on intellectual development.[3] Since the mid-1980s Gardner's theory has been applied in educational contexts and there has been a growing MI school movement in the USA and elsewhere.

The Education Department at University College Cork is currently undertaking a research project[4] to examine the application of the theory of Multiple Intelligences to pedagogy and assessment in an Irish context. The project aims to use an MI framework to develop teaching and learning strategies as well as modes and techniques of assessment. The project addresses three specific areas: the transition from primary to second-level schooling, Civic, Social and Political Education and the Transition Year Programme. It is hoped that developments in these areas will ultimately have potential for transferability to other curricular areas.

Theory of Multiple Intelligences

The Theory of Multiple Intelligence was first proposed by Gardner in 1983 in

Frames of Mind[5] as a direct challenge to the "classical view of intelligence".[6] Gardner was not the first to challenge the view that intelligence is a "unitary capacity for logical reasoning of the sort exemplified by mathematicians, scientists, and logicians."[7] As far back as 1938, L.L. Thurstone asserted that human intellect "encompasses several mental abilities".[8] In an Irish context, Kathleen Lynch has suggested that the greatest single constraint in Irish education is "the narrow and scientifically untenable conception of ability" which underpins it.[9] Intelligence is understood as a fixed entity which does not change over time, is defined in narrow linguistic/logical terms, and is widely held to be measurable by an IQ score.[10]

Frames of Mind did not attract much attention within its own discipline but aroused considerable interest among the general public and professional educators.[11] Reflecting ten years later on his decision to write about "intelligences" rather than "talents", Gardner states:

> Had I simply noted that human beings possess different talents, this claim would have been uncontroversial - and my book would have gone unmentioned. But I made a deliberate decision to write about "multiple intelligences": "multiple" to stress an unknown number of separate human capacities, ranging from musical intelligence to the intelligence involved in understanding oneself; "intelligence" to underscore that these capacities were as fundamental as those historically captured within the IQ test.[12]

Preliminary findings from the Multiple Intelligence, Curriculum and Assessment project in UCC suggest that there is little resistance to describing particular individual capacities as "talents", "gifts", or "aptitudes", but that people tend to be reluctant to move away from traditional constructs of "intelligence".

Gardner's theory of Multiple Intelligences

Gardner defines an intelligence as the "ability to solve problems or fashion products that are of consequence in a particular cultural setting or community".[13] The problem-solving skill allows one to approach a situation in which a goal is to be obtained and to locate the appropriate route to that goal.[14] According to Gardner, there are at least eight[15] relatively autonomous but interconnected intelligences.[16] Gardner bases his claims for the existence of at least eight intelligences on psychological, neuropsychological, neuro-biological historical and evolutionary evidence as well as on findings from psychological experimental tasks.

Some characteristics of the intelligences together with end-states[17] that exemplify them are described in Table 1 below. This table offers an outline map of the topography of what is a complex theory. It neither exemplifies nor exhausts that theory. Its value is illustrative only. Used as a template in the classroom, it might unintentionally give rise to practices which would be dangerously reductive.[18] It is useful to remember that Gardner views intelligence as a term for organising and describing human capabilities, rather than "a reference to some commodity inside the head".[19] According to Kornhaber and Gardner, intelligence is not a "thing", but rather… a potential, the presence of which allows an individual access to forms of thinking appropriate to specific kinds of content'.[20]

Table 1   Multiple Intelligences: Description and End States[21]

INTELLIGENCE	DESCRIPTION	EXEMPLIFIED BY
Linguistic	involves the capacity to use language to express and appreciate complex meanings	poets, lawyers, journalists
Logical -Mathematical	involves using and appreciating abstract relations	mathematicians, scientists computer programmers, accountants, engineers
Spatial	concerns the ability to perceive visual or spatial information, to transform and modify this information, and to recreate visual images even without reference to an original physical stimulus	artists, geographers, surgeons, pilots, architects, navigators, hunters
Bodily-Kinaesthetic	involves the use of all or part of one's body to solve problems, fashion products, construct meaning	dancers, choreographers, actors, athletes, rock climbers, surgeons
Musical	allows people to create, communicate, and understand meanings made out of sound	composers, conductors, instrumentalists, audio engineers

Naturalist	concerns the ability to recognise and understand categories in one's environment	botanists, biologists
Interpersonal	ability to perceive and make distinctions in the moods, intentions, motivations and feelings of other people and to act accordingly	psychiatrists, religious leaders, teachers, diplomats
Intrapersonal	enables individuals to know their own abilities and perceive how to best use them	elders in a community, novelists, poets

Gardner established a number of criteria which had to be satisfied before a particular observable faculty might be classified as a discrete intelligence. Evidence from the following sources was considered:

> knowledge about normal development and development in gifted individuals; information about the breakdown of cognitive skills under conditions of brain damage; studies of exceptional populations, including prodigies, *idiots savants,* and autistic children; data about the evolution of cognition over the millennia; cross-cultural accounts of cognition; psychometric studies, including examinations of correlations among tests; and psychological training studies, particularly measures of transfer and generalisation across tasks... In addition to satisfying (these) criteria, each intelligence must have an identifiable core operation or set of operations... An intelligence must also be susceptible to encoding in a symbol system - a culturally contrived system of meaning, which captures and conveys important forms of information.[22]

MI and related areas

A number of areas of specific relevance to education have arisen from work on Multiple Intelligences. These include research on thinking dispositions, learning styles, and the place of the arts in education. MI scholarship has provided the seed-bed for the development of the *Teaching for Understanding* (TfU) model). The confluence of MI theory and a TfU model raises interesting questions about assessment practices. The interrogation of assessment practice has emerged as a central issue and has generated work in the area of *Authentic Assessment* including Portfolio assessment. If learners learn in different ways, then it makes sense for them to illustrate understanding in different ways. Portfolio assessment, which embraces a range of practices in which classroom work, fieldwork, homework, *etc.* may be integrated, allows for this. Already the subject of an interesting literature, the UCC project hopes to contribute to developments in this area. While detailed discussion of assessment issues is outside the scope of this paper, engagement with these is essential in informing and enriching MI practice at classroom, school or system level.

Intelligence profiles and comfort zones

The recognition of a multiplicity of intelligences requires that recognition of the developmental potential of a diversity of learner styles and teaching styles must now be factored into the teaching-learning equation. Both learners and teachers have a range of intelligence profiles. Intelligence profiles tend to be jagged and so one finds in any group of people, many diverse profiles. In any classroom one may find twenty or thirty intelligence profiles. As a general rule people tend to operate out of "comfort zones". This means that we tend to feel most at ease in the intelligence areas where we are strong. In classrooms where student intelligence profiles match teacher intelligence profiles, it would appear to follow that as teachers are teaching through intelligence areas where they are strong and students are learning through areas of relative strength, it is likely that learning is taking place with some ease. When a mismatch occurs, however, problems may arise. If teachers teach consistently or exclusively through intelligence areas where only some students are strong then many students may be struggling to learn in ways which suit neither their learning styles nor intelligence profiles.

MI into Practice

These questions presented themselves as seminal issues to the MI project team at UCC. Two remedies suggested themselves and were subsequently formulated into exercises in professional development, as follows:

1. Teachers were encouraged to identify their own intelligence profiles and to begin to examine whether some intelligence areas might be more dominant than others in their classrooms. That done, they were asked to consider whether it might be possible to distribute teaching approaches more evenly

across the intelligences. This identification could either be done in conjunction with or as a prelude to identifying student intelligence profiles.

2. Teachers were asked to consider the use of a number of "entry points" when approaching the teaching of a topic. Gardner suggests that any rich, nourishing topic - any concept worth teaching - can be approached in a least five different ways. He suggests thinking of the topic as a room with at least five doors or entry points into it. "Students vary as to which entry point is most appropriate for them and which routes are most comfortable to follow once they have gained initial access to the room".23 The entry points map roughly onto the intelligences and are as follows:

- the narrational,
- aesthetic,
- logical-quantitative,
- foundational and
- experiential.

The *narrational* entry point present a story or narrative about the concept in question. The *aesthetic* entry point emphasises sensory or surface features which will appeal to learners who favour an artistic stance to the experiences of living. The *logical-quantitative* involves approaching the topic through deductive reasoning processes or through invoking numerical considerations. The *foundational* entry point examines philosophical and terminological facets of the concept and is appropriate for people who like to pose fundamental questions "of the sort that one associates with young children and with philosophers rather than with more practical (or more 'middle aged') spirits.24 Finally, the *experimental* entry point is appropriate for those who learn best with a 'handshake' approach, dealing directly with the materials that embody or convey the concept.

In underlining the importance of using a variety of entry points, Gardner writes:

In one definition, a skilled teacher is a person who can open a number of different windows on the same concept... An effective teacher functions as a 'student-curriculum-broker', ever vigilant for educational prosthetics -

texts, film, software - that can help convey the relevant contents, in as engaging and effective a way as possible, to students who exhibit a characteristic learning mode.[25]

He goes on to say:

It should be evident that use of multiple entry points can be a powerful means of dealing with student misconceptions, biases, and stereotypes. So long as one takes only a single perspective or tack on a concept or problem, it is virtually certain that students will understand that concept in only the most limited and rigid fashion. Conversely, the adoption of a family of stances towards a phenomenon encourages the student to come to know that phenomenon in more than one way, to develop multiple representations and seek to relate these representations to one another.[26]

I have quoted at some length from Gardner on entry points for three reasons. Firstly, the use of entry points illustrates the possibilities of teaching *through* the intelligences, which *ipso facto* lends to teaching *for* the intelligences. Once familiar with the entry points, such an approach may be considered in any topic for any subject area.

Secondly, and more importantly, it is essential to clarify that a Multiple Intelligences approach to teaching and learning derives from a sophisticated and complex theory of mind and intelligence. Accordingly, classroom practices which set out to harness MI insights in order to enable more learning and better learning must respond to this. While strategies which enact MI insights are of course within the compass of every teacher and any learner, the application of MI in classrooms must not be misrepresented as a matter of assembling and dipping into "a new bag of tricks" merely to enliven the implementation of already existing structures of subject-based knowledge.

Finally, MI theory should not be summoned to privilege any particular set of teaching methods which are alleged to be somehow appropriate to all learners and to all teachers, at all times. An example of the unfortunate consequences which might result from ignoring this warning would be the classroom where exclusive use of text-based teacher narration and learner passivity is replaced by an all-out commitment to high-energy physical activity with musical accompaniment.[27] MI theory has not declared war on the text, for instance. Applying MI to classrooms enables us to understand that texts exist within more complex matrices of understanding than one might imagine from an analysis of conventional teacher/learner relationships frozen in the inflexible stare of the terminal examination.

Conclusion

MI approaches call for a fundamental appraisal/re-appraisal of how we view intelligence and potential in relation to *all* our students. Such re-appraisal is within the scope of every teacher and every school. Good schools and effective teachers carry out many re-evaluations of their own effectiveness every day. Gardner's theory applied to school contexts provides a flexible and challenging lens through which to conceptualise such ongoing professional acts. MI theory is also a tool for change, and it is important to recognise the need to commit to its insistence on *taking action* arising out of (re-) appraisal. Such action would include supporting practices which recognise diversity and plurality in student learning as well as in teacher style. Colleagues will appreciate the urgency of the consequent need to find diverse and pluralist approaches to assessing student performance. The UCC MI, Curriculum and Assessment project is deeply committed to engaging with the implications of applied MI theory for pedagogy and assessment *in an Irish context,* not least in relation to ongoing professional development for teachers.

1 Gardner, H., Kornhaber, M.L., Wake, W.K. (1996), *Intelligence - Multiple Perspectives,* Fort Worth: Harcourt Brace. pvii

2 Sternberg R.J. (1990), *Metaphors of Mind - Conceptions of the Nature of Intelligence,* Canada: Cambridge University Press. p261. Sternberg defines the systems metaphor as "an attempt to bring together various other metaphors by viewing intelligence in terms of a complex interaction of various cognitive and other systems".

3 Sternberg, R.J. (1990)

4 A report on Phase I of the UCC project (October 1995 to September 1996) is available from the Education Department, UCC. Phase II of the project runs from October 1996 to May 1999. The project steering committee is chaired by Professor Áine Hyland. The project director is Dr. Joan Hanafin. Two Research Fellows and two Research Assistants currently work full-time on the project. Thirty teachers (primary and second-level) are investigating the application of MI theory at the transition from primary to second-level schooling. Fifteen second-level teachers are involved in a pilot using MI theory in the teaching and assessing of Civic, Social and Political Education. Project activities include staff development

initiatives, information sessions, seminars, a summer school, production of materials including MI strategies, approaches to lesson planning *etc.*

5 Gardner, H. (1983). *Frames of Minds: The Theory of Multiple Intelligences.* New York: Harper and Row. 2nd ed. (1993) London: Fontana Press

6 Gardner, H. *et al.,* (1996), pp202-203

7 *ibid.* p203

8 *ibid.* p203

9 Lynch, K. (1988), "Developing Abilities: What Are We Doing in Second-Level Education at Present?", *Compass,* Vol.17, No.2, pp.47-60, Dublin: IACD. p52

10 Fontes, P. and Kellaghan, T. (1983) "Opinions of the Irish public on intelligence", *The Irish Journal of Education,* Vol. XVII, No. 2, pp55-67 cited in Lynch (1988)

11 Gardner, H. (1993), *Multiple Intelligences - The Theory in Practice,* New York: Basic Books, pxii

12 *ibid.,* pxi-xii

13 *ibid.,* p15

14 *ibid.* Gardner goes on "The creation of a *cultural* product is crucial to such functions as capturing and transmitting knowledge or expressing one's views or feelings. The problems to be solved range from creating an end for a story to anticipating a mating move in chess to repairing a quilt. Products range from scientific theories to musical compositions to successful political campaigns." p15

15 The eighth intelligence which has been recently proposed, *viz.,* a naturalist intelligence, is described as "the kind of skill at recognising flora and fauna that one associates with biologists like Darwin". Gardner H. (1995). "Reflections on multiple intelligences: Myths and messages', *Phi Delta Kappan,* 77(2)

16 Gardner has suggested recently that there is some evidence for a ninth intelligence, an existential or spiritual intelligence.

17 Gardner emphasises that all endstates draw on *combinations* of several intelligences, Gardner *et al.* (1996), p211

18 See footnote 27

19 Gardner, H. *et al.* (1996), p205

20 Kornhaber and Gardner, 1991, p155 cited in Gardner, H. *et al.* (1996), p205

21 This table was compiled using Gardner, H. *et al.* (1996) pp205-211, Gardner H. (1993), and Campbell, B. (1994) *The Multiple Intelligences Handbook.* Stanwood: Campbell & Assoc., Inc.

22 Gardner, H. (1993) p16

23 *ibid.* pp203-204

24 *ibid.* p203

25 *ibid.* p204

26 *ibid.* pp204-5

27 See footnote 18

GENDER AND THE JUNIOR CERTIFICATE

MARY DUGGAN AND CARMEL HENEGHAN

The introduction of the Junior Certificate programme marked a major development in Irish education. It aimed at providing a single unified programme for 12-15 year olds, the aims and principles of which are set out in the N.C.C.A. "A programme for reform" as follows:

The Junior Certificate programme aims to -

- Reinforce and further develop in the young person the knowledge, understanding, attitudes, skills and competencies acquired at primary level.
- Extend and deepen the range and quality of the young person's educational experience in terms of knowledge, understanding, attitudes, skills and competencies.
- Develop the young person's personal and social confidence, initiative and competence through a broad well balanced general education.
- Prepare the young person for the requirements of further programmes of study, of employment or of life outside full education.
- Contribute to the moral and spiritual development of the young person and develop a tolerance and respect for the values and beliefs of others.
- Prepare the young person for the responsibilities of citizenship in the national context and in the context of the wider European and global communities.

Curriculum Principles

The Junior Certificate programme is based on the following curriculum principles:

- **Breadth and Balance:** In the final phase of compulsory schooling every young person should have a wide range of educational experiences. Particular attention must be given to reinforcing and developing the skills of numeracy, literacy and oracy.
- **Relevance:** Curriculum provision should address the immediate and prospective needs of the young person, in the context of the cultural,

economic and social environment.

- **Quality:** Every young person should be challenged to achieve the highest possible standards of excellence with due regard to different aptitudes and abilities and to international comparisons.
- **Continuity and Progression:** Education should be seen as a continuum with close alignment between the primary level and the junior cycle post-primary level in curriculum learning processes and teaching methods. Progression should take account of the developing needs of the young person and the changing teaching and learning environment towards the end of the period of compulsory education.
- **Coherence:** The curriculum should provide a coherent and consistent educational experience for young people through a broad, balanced programme with appropriate depth of treatment while encouraging young people to make connections between the different areas of educational experience.

While all the above pertains to both genders the only *specific* mention of gender equity in the report is under "Implementing the curriculum framework" where it is stated that "the curriculum framework should apply in planning the curriculum for all students, irrespective of such variables as *gender,* ability, aptitude or geographical location".

In this paper we propose to look at some gender differences pertaining to the Junior Cycle.

Flexibility in the Curriculum

"While retaining the practice of centrally defined courses designed for implementation nationally, a great degree of flexibility is offered to schools and teachers in the interpretation and development of (these) courses." (N.C.C.A. report). This theory is invaluable in allowing for programmes which will "contribute towards the development of all aspects of the individual" and should allow for progress in all areas - not least in the area of gender equity. The practice, however, can be very different. School principals while seeing curriculum development as an integral part of their job, constantly bemoan the fact that due to an almost complete absence of the support structure they cannot devote the time necessary for such development (Principals sub-committee 1995/96). It is not surprising, therefore, that gender equity often gets forgotten about when subject provision, teacher allocation, departmental requirements etc. are catered for on very meagre resources.

"A conscious attempt is made in the Junior Certificate programme to identify areas of linkage between different subjects. Common themes and issues are often treated in different but complementary ways" (N.C.C.A.). This is a rational, even laudable approach. Its effectiveness, however, depends on subject teachers co-ordinating their programmes and working in close co-operation with each other. This may seem perfectly reasonable to the Department of Education (and the Futures Pack is a fine production aimed at promoting such co-ordination and co-operation) but, as we have seen before and since the introduction of the Junior Certificate, no cognisance was taken of the *time* required to implement such co-ordination. Teachers were expected, after two days inservice, to familiarise themselves with new material and draw up courses using the "local community and environment as a teaching/learning resource." An ideal opportunity existed to bring about some real change but it is little wonder that many teachers - faced with large classes, a full workload, no provision for cross-curricular planning - and keeping in mind that "every young person should be challenged to achieve the highest possible standards of excellence" - stick with tried and trusted pedagogical methods and subject material and have little time to consider gender in their particular disciplines.

Classroom Interaction

There is substantial evidence internationally that teachers - even those well disposed towards equality - interact differently with their male and female pupils and this operates to the disadvantage of the female pupils. (Drudy and Lynch). Research done at primary level (Paris O.E.C.D. 1986) concludes that boys are the focus of attention in mixed-sex classrooms. Observations in classrooms at second-level in many countries have shown that boys both demand and get more teacher attention (Asken and Ross 1988) (Wilson 1991). A substantial amount of this is in the form of disciplinary interventions - reprimanding the boys for their behaviour. Boys of all ages also receive more praise from both female and male teachers even though teachers are adamant that they do not give more attention to the boys than to girls (Kaiser 1991) (Drudy & Lynch). British studies found that teachers often exploit rivalry between the sexes to motivate or manage pupils. There is evidence to suggest that they deliberately gear the context of lessons towards boys' interests in order to retain attention and control whereas girls remain "passive" in class. (Wilson 1991).

Research with Irish trainee teachers at second-level indicated similar tendencies. Boys were asked significantly more questions than girls. As a result girls were asked fewer higher cognitive questions and were less intellectually challenged (Drudy & Lynch). Hence the need for inservice training for teachers at both Junior and Senior cycle in pedagogical practices regarding gender equity.

Otherwise "girls will continue to be presented with a dual role model - on the one hand they are educated to compete and succeed within the formal education system: on the other hand they are socialised to be guardians of the moral order and non-assertive. Boys are not presented with this dichotomous model. Entry into employment is encouraged in a much more single minded way" (Drudy).

Sexism/Stereotyping in Texts

There cannot be real equality of education provision unless there is a real effort to oppose sexism or stereotyping wherever either exists. Clear messages about equality should be given through all books and materials used in the classroom and positive role models should be provided for all young people.

How do the texts used by Junior Certificate students in your school measure up?

Checklist
- How many novels, plays, short stories are chosen in Gaeilge or English with girls or women as the main characters?
- How many women authors are featured?
- Are sexist/stereotypical illustrations used in teaching materials?
- Are women role models to be found in text books in subjects like science, geography or history?

Even a very quick comparison between the texts used today and those used 10-15 years ago will show that we have come a long way in this area, although their is still some way to go particularly with regard to female authors.

A study of some of the texts most widely used revealed the following

Gaeilge

Poems	Text 1	Text 2	Text 3	Text 4
Male Authors	22	20	24	17
Female Authors	2	–	3	6
Anon.	1	1	3	1
Prose				
Male	–	–	6	15
Female	–	–	3	2
Anon.	–	–	1	–

ENGLISH

Poetry	Text 1	Text 2	Text 3
Male	30	25	80
Female	3	7	26
Anon.	–	–	–

Prose			
Male	15	9	–
Female	3	3	–
Anon.	–	–	–

It is fair to say that due to the flexibility of the curriculum the individual teacher has the freedom to select a balance of both male and female authors. However, there is a strong temptation for the overworked teacher to stay with the text, as researching alternative material is time consuming and is essential for other courses such as Transition Year and the Leaving Cert. Applied.

Science:

An analysis of 158 illustrations - mostly cartoon and photograph, found that 118 of them related to male and 40 related to females.

When one allows for the fact that 28 male inventors/ discovers are included - a fact which could not be balanced as the vast majority of inventors were men there is still an imbalance in number.

This however is of little importance in our view as the men and women featured are involved in a wide variety of pursuits and experiments and there is no obvious gender stereotyping.

Home Economics:

This analysis covered 155 illustrations and found that 85 related to males and 70 to females.

As with the science text there is no gender stereotyping as men and women are pictured in caring and domestic roles; both are also involved in sport and scientific experiments. The only chapter (in one book) featuring one gender (female) exclusively is Fashion and Design.

Technical Graphics

The language in texts is gender neutral and the graphics are generally balanced. As with Home Economics the gender uptake is still very traditional.

History

As history is a core subject in secondary schools and one which gives students an overview of their place in society, it merits, we feel, a more in-depth consideration - especially as women have been all but "written out" of history.

The Junior Cert history syllabus includes a technical evaluation of the role of the historian and the application of those skills, from ancient civilisations through the Middle Ages to Modern times; it suggests an evaluation of social history in its proper context. Within this framework there is ample scope for equal treatment of women's contribution to society. Sadly there is a dearth of such contributions - many are ignored and some are treated superficially.

In ancient society the country was not deemed safe unless the King had mated with the pagan goddess who symbolised fertility suggesting an equal role for the female. Some women occupied an important role in society as exemplified in the myth regarding the pagan goddess Bridget - transformed into Bridget Patron saint of Ireland and Abbess of Kildare. Even the Bishop was under the jurisdiction of the Abbess. These stories are not included in the syllabus.

Joan of Arc liberated her country from English tyranny and was betrayed. She was denied recognition until her canonisation this century. There is no mention of her role in the section dealing with the Middle Ages. Peter the Great is credited with beginning the process of civilising and modernising Russia. Catherine the Great played no small part in developing the process - nevertheless she was banded as sexually licentious - a trait not regarded as negative in men at the time.

Florence Nightingale pioneered hygienic standards in hospitals which saved thousands of lives. She received little recognition until her old age when she was awarded The Order of Merit. Unfortunately the services and achievements of the "Lady with the Lamp" do not enrich our Junior Cert syllabus.

Lady Gregory played a vital role in the Literary Revival. However attention is focused on Yeats and Synge. None of the Junior Cert text books highlight the role of women in this period.

Countess Markievicz was deeply involved in the Irish Citizen Army. Little credit is given to her as James Connolly and James Larkin are given prominence in the history texts. She was the first woman elected to the House of Commons and the first female cabinet minister in Dail Eireann. Despite her achievements she is accorded but a grudging mention in the Junior Cert. course.

The Suffragettes, a significant movement which won landmark rights for women, are not discussed in depth. These women were force-fed, maltreated and abused for demanding rights. Their contribution was immense yet their treatment in the Junior Cert course is superficial.

Maude Gonne Mac Bride played an important role in "Cumann na mBan". This organisation together with "Iníonacha na hEireann' and "Ladies Landleague" and other women's movements do not feature in the course. The young generation of today are deprived of an enriching and balanced post.

Gender Differences in Subject Choice
A survey published by the N.C.C.A. in 1994 showed that a greater number of females took 6 or more subjects at Higher level. 15.49% of females compared with 11.54% of males took 8 Higher level papers. On the other hand 16.32% of males compared with 10.60% of females took no examination at the Higher level. The tendency for male candidates to take fewer Higher level papers had increased since 1992. In the core subjects, differences between the proportions of male and female candidates who chose the subjects are not great - for obvious reasons. The greatest differences here occur in Science (where 52.80% of candidates were male) and History where 51.78% of candidates were female). Gender bias becomes more obvious in the subjects that come next in order of popularity. Almost 56% of candidates were female in the case of both French and Business Studies. Home Economics where 90.95% of candidates were female and Music (78.95% female), are still largely female preserves. There has been an increase (ranging from 2 - 8 %) in male participation in these subjects since 1992. At the other extreme, Technical Graphics, Materials Technology and Metalwork remain male preserves - 91.11%, 92.84% and 95.35% male candidates respectively. These subjects show an increase in female participation of between 1-2 percentage points since 1992.

Examination Results: Gender Differences in Grades
Throughout subjects in general, at all three levels, Foundation, Ordinary and Higher, a higher proportion of females than males obtained high grades (A&B). At higher level, 41.68% of females compared with 35.66% of males obtained an A or B grade. At the other extreme a higher proportion of males than females were awarded low grades (E.F.NG.) 5.85% v. 3.38% at higher level. When one examines the results for individual subjects at the higher level, one finds that for all major subjects, with the exception of Mathematics (4.71%

As among males and 3.42% As among females) and subjects which were predominantly taken by boys (Materials Technology (wood)), Metalwork, Technical Graphics) a greater proportion of girls than boys achieved A grades. A similar picture emerges for B grades except for Mathematics, in which girls do better than boys (35.83% female, 31.51% male). At Ordinary level a female advantage in A and B grades is also in evidence. The findings are similar to high level, except that a greater proportion of girls than of boys achieved high grades (A and B) in Mathematics and male superiority in subjects taken predominantly by boys was dented by the larger proportion of girls who were awarded an A in Materials Technology (wood) (2.07% v 1.63%).

At Foundation level, a higher proportion of girls than of boys achieved high grades (A and B) in Gaeilge and English. A larger proportion of boys achieved A grades in Mathematics, but a slightly larger proportion of girls achieved B grades.

Factors Influencing Exam Performance
Socioeconomic Factors
The E.S.R.I. report on Co-education and Gender Equality shows that a number of measures of parental socioeconomic status have a significant impact on grade point average. Family background factors explain 13% of the variance between pupils within schools: a result of the differing social backgrounds of their pupils. Pupils from lower social backgrounds have a lower grade point average than those from the higher classes: daughters (but not sons) of farmers have a higher GPA than others and attending school in the west of Ireland also has a significant positive effect.

Social background factors appear to have a stronger influence on the exam performance of girls than of boys. Only location in the west of Ireland and birth order (eldest and older children doing best) have a more marked effect on boys than girls.

Coed or Single Sex
The same report shows that coeducation has little or no effect on Junior Certificate performance when differences in social background, ability and school organisation are taken into account. Coeducation per se explains less than one percent of the average difference between schools in overall exam results. The impact is strongest among lower ability pupils, where boys in coeducational schools do somewhat better and girls do slightly worse than their counterparts in single-sex schools. (The grade point average of boys in this category was boosted by boys in vocational schools taking more practical

subjects than their single-sex counterparts). In contrast, co-education has no impact on middle and higher ability pupils.

Girls in single sex schools have a more positive attitude to maths than girls in coeducational schools and this has a negative effect on the performance of girls in coeducational schools - a difference of half a grade above their counterparts in single-sex schools.

Academic Self-Image
This was found to be closely related to the nature of feedback given to the pupils. Pupils were found to have more confidence in their abilities when they had positive interaction with their teachers and where teacher and parental expectations were high. Girls tend to have lower academic self-images than their male counterparts: coeducation has no significant impact on girls in this regard but tends to make boys at Junior Cert level somewhat more self-critical of their abilities.

Levels of psycho-social stress are much higher among Junior and Leaving Cert pupils than among young adults or older people. Aspects of the schooling process, such as quality of the relationships with teachers and other pupils, were shown to have a strong influence on stress levels.

Streaming
Streaming was found to have a negative (but statistically insignificant) impact on the *average* performance of pupils; controlling for other factors, pupils in schools where classes were mixed ability scored just under half a grade higher than pupils in rigidly streamed schools. Streaming became statistically significant when academic ability was entered into the model. Allocation to streamed/banded classes increased GPA for those in the top class but depressed GPA for those in the bottom class, even when the pupils were of similar ability. There were several possible explanations for this pattern. Firstly, bottom class were more likely to be allocated ordinary (or foundation) level subjects which, in turn, impacted on pupils' GPA. Secondly, a slower pace of instruction in bottom classes may have resulted in a less complete coverage of the curriculum (Pallas et al 1994). Thirdly, a peer culture opposed to the academic ethos may have emerged within a class labelled as "less able" (Willis 1977).

Homework
Pupils tend to do better in schools where there are clear rules about carrying out and checking of homework, and where these rules are backed up by

sanctions: however while positive for both boys and girls the results were significant only for girls.

Conclusions

The Junior Certificate programme offers scope for a creative approach towards nurturing the individual and thereby contributing to economic and social well being. However, while teachers may welcome the freedom which the Junior Cert course gives them there is no doubt that this flexibility has a downside. Planning new courses is time consuming and the "ready-made" set of questions is no longer at one's fingertips. The aims and principles as set down are laudable but there are clear staffing and resourcing implications if the curricular framework is to be implemented adequately in all schools.

It is disappointing that despite efforts to present subjects (through texts etc) in a gender friendly manner and despite efforts to promote "subject sampling" in first year, there are still considerable gender differences in participation in subjects traditionally associated with gender. This supports the view that factors, (other than course content and presentation) such as school organisation and ethos, parental attitudes and traditional role models, play a significant part in subject choice.

The relative lack of ambition and under achievement of boys, which is apparent from the gender differences in grades, is a worrying trend meriting urgent investigation. Girls' negative attitude to and relative underachievement in Maths must also be addressed sooner rather than later.

Whether gender equality is considered at all in the school and in the classroom depends on the extent to which the principal and staff are conscious of the need for its promotion.

Recommendations

The E.R.S.I. report states the following:
- The state should take a more proactive role in promoting gender and class equality objectives among schools and local school systems - as well as *developing effective policy instruments to ensure their implementation.*
- Schools should develop their own gender equality policies, focusing on the personal and social development of pupils as well as on the take ups and performance in non-traditional subjects.

The A.S.T.I. Model Policy on Gender Equality makes the following recommendations to school managers.

The school's Board of Management should:

- Make arrangements for appropriate incareer/inservice training for the principal.
- Make arrangements for appropriate incareer/inservice training for staff.
- Include both genders in the management and decision making structures of the school.

The school should endeavour to ensure that:
- Girls and boys have access to subject sampling in first year.
- Timetabling arrangements are designed to enable boys and girls to select "non traditional" subjects. (Traditional subjects should not be set against each other - ie Home Economics/Technical Graphics)
- Girls and boys have equal access to the full range of curricular options.
- Gender related issues are highlighted across the curriculum in all subject areas.
- Time is provided for inservice modules for staff to review classroom management techniques.

THE INTEGRATION OF PUPILS WITH DISABILITIES INTO MAINSTREAM EDUCATION AT SECOND LEVEL

MICHAEL SHEVLIN

"The key concern would be to enable each pupil to discover the nature and scope of his or her particular potentials and limitations; to enable each and every pupil to make the most of these potentials; to overcome limitations wherever this is possible; to mitigate their effects wherever it is not." (Report on the National Education Convention, 1994, p.8).

The philosophy of education encapsulated in this statement has received widespread acceptance within the educational community. It promotes an optimistic view of education wherein the capacity of each child to develop his/her potential is emphasised. Ensuring that young people avail of the opportunity to develop their full potential is the critical task facing all educators. The task is essentially the same where young people with disabilities are concerned. Enabling these young people to gain access to the richness of educational development should be an integral element of any country's educational provision.

In this article a brief review of the current thinking on the integration of pupils with disabilities into mainstream schools will be discussed. The barriers to the full participation of these pupils in the educational system will be outlined. Finally ways of meeting the challenge of including pupils with disabilities in mainstream schools will be suggested.

Special Education - The Traditional View

Traditionally, special education has been perceived as the specialised wing of the educational system which catered for those with disabilities (Ainscow, 1989). Young people with a disability had been considered to be ineducatable.

Gradually, provision developed for those with sensory or physical disabilities while facilities for the intellectually disabled lagged far behind. Educators contended that disabled people would benefit from access to a unique body of knowledge (Flynn and Kowalczyk - McPhee, 1989). Specially designed curricula were developed by specially trained teachers who employed specialist techniques. Education was usually provided on the basis of category of disability and separate provision was the logical outcome given that mainstream schools appeared unable to cater for these children. As result parallel systems of special and mainstream education developed in many countries including Ireland (McGee, 1990).

Changing Perspectives

Over the past twenty years a radical reappraisal of what constitutes special education has occurred. Previously entrenched assumptions about the capabilities of people with disabilities have been challenged. In the past, special institutions had been created to protect and care for disabled people. Medical and psychological perspectives dominated the discourse about disability (Barton, 1996). Improving the functional capacities of individuals formed the focus of habilitative services (Habin, 1987, Halliday, 1993).

Advocates of normalisation and integration were highly critical of this approach as it isolated and marginalised disabled people. Enabling people with disabilities to live with their families in their local communities with whatever supports they required was the central tenet of the normalisation movement which had originated in Scandinavia. The integration movement was based on the perception that disabled people had the right to participate fully in society. Access to mainstream schools was considered an integral element in providing an equalisation of opportunities for people with disabilities (UNESCO, 1994). This would involve the creation of a fairer world wherein difference would be understood and diversity valued.

Another salient factor in this fundamental reappraisal of special educational provision was the realisation that substantial numbers of pupils were failing to benefit from the education offered in mainstream schools. The Warnock Report (1978) confirmed this observation when it concluded that anything up to 20% of the school population may encounter serious difficulties in learning. These 20% of the school population were often classified under the labels of 'slow learners' or 'difficult to teach' (Westwood, 1995). It was gradually realised that within-child factors were not the sole reasons for the learning difficulties experienced. Learning difficulties originated from a complex interaction of factors within the individual child combined with factors from the child's environment. Educators began to examine the influence of the school on learning outcomes. It was discovered that school organisation, curriculum content, pedagogy and teacher expectations of individual pupils had a profound influence on learning outcomes.

The concept of special educational provision was reformulated to include pupils with disabilities within mainstream settings and to review existing arrangements for pupils with special needs attending mainstream schools.

Barriers to full participation:
Translating the principle of integration into reality has proved difficult. Few practical guidelines exist to enable schools to develop inclusive approaches for pupils with disabilities. School responses to pupils with disabilities vary considerably and it is difficult to discern an overall pattern.

What is not difficult to discern are the problems schools encounter in providing effectively for pupils with special needs within their current framework. These difficulties represent one of the most serious obstacles to the full participation of pupils with disabilities within mainstream settings. Recent reports have identified the factors which inhibit the effective delivery of special educational provision (Government of Ireland, 1993; Government of Ireland, 1996). These include lack of information on educational options and entitlements, paucity of resources, negative attitudes and the lack of appropriate curricula to facilitate individual needs.

Individual teachers have reported a series of difficulties in responding adequately to pupils with special needs within the classroom (Lynch, 1995). They candidly admit their lack of knowledge and expertise which inhibit an effective response to individual learning difficulties. Attempting to create a flexible classroom structure and access to the curriculum for pupils of varying needs and abilities presented particular problems. In their opinion, the paucity of inservice provision, the inadequacy of support services and the failure to disseminate models of good practice exacerbated an already difficult situation.

Meeting the Challenge:
Before the 1960's, people with disabilities were regarded as quite different from the rest of the population in many countries. For many, ordinary schooling was not an option and their capacity to benefit from education was questioned (Hegarty, 1993a). These perceptions no longer apply. To an increasing extent pupils who have physical, sensory or intellectual disabilities

are joining their peers who traditionally encountered difficulties in learning within mainstream settings. The latest figures (Government of Ireland, 1993; Government of Ireland, 1996) appear to confirm this trend. Some 3,800 pupils with various disabilities are in special classes at primary level with approximately 2,300 pupils in 48 special classes at post-primary level. The five designated post-primary schools have another 100 pupils enrolled. In ordinary classes at primary level there are an estimated 8,000 pupils with "specific disabilities". Approximately 8,000 pupils with disabilities, the majority intellectual, attend 114 Special Schools. People who have a disability demand the same rights and opportunities in education as everyone else. Educating pupils with disabilities in mainstream settings gives them the opportunity to learn how to live and work with their peers in an integrated environment.

Including pupils who have disabilities within mainstream schools requires the construction of a coherent system for the delivery of special educational provision. At a systemic level enabling legislation, a special needs advisory service and developing links between mainstream and special schools could ameliorate many of the difficulties encountered in creating a comprehensive system of special educational provision.

Enabling legislation would contain four essential elements: affirming the right of all pupils with disabilities to an appropriate education within their own community whenever possible; asserting the responsibility of all schools to accommodate this right where feasible; securing resources from the state for all schools catering for pupils with disabilities; according the right to appeal to parent(s) who feel his/her child is not being given access to appropriate education (O'Murchú, 1996).

A special needs advisory service, (Ainscow and Muncey, 1989) could enable schools to respond more effectively to pupils who have disabilities by:

(a) providing information about available resources, and approaches to special needs provision for parents, teachers, pupils with a disability and school managements.

(b) enabling a 'whole school' approach to be developed when devising a school policy, implementing identification and assessment procedures and delivering educational provision for pupils with disabilities and/or special needs.

(c) co-ordinating the available support services (educational, psychological, medical) to provide a coherent response to pupils with disabilities and/or special needs.

(d) developing modular in-service programmes to support school personnel.

(e) disseminating examples of good practice.

Pupils who have disabilities are a heterogeneous group and categories of disability are often meaningless when linked to the type of educational provision required by an individual child. The Special Needs Advisory Service could enable each school to develop policies and practices which are compatible with the individual needs of the disabled pupils in attendance.

Bridging the parallel systems of mainstream and special education could make a valuable contribution to the integration of pupils with disabilities into mainstream schools (Jowett et al., 1988). In England and Wales link programmes between mainstream and special schools have developed which provide access to a broader curriculum and present opportunities for co-operative learning for pupils with and without disabilities (Beveridge, 1996, Whitaker, 1994). Teachers from both types of schools have benefited from the exchange of ideas, the acquisition of new skills and the shared planning of a joint curriculum (Fletcher-Campbell, 1994). Similar developments are taking place in Ireland though not on such an extensive scale. A shared curriculum in Art, Music, Physical Education, Drama, Dance and Home Economics has been developed through the Fast Friends link programmes (Walsh et al., 1996).

These link programmes provide models of good practice which could be usefully expanded to encompass a joint approach to meeting the needs of pupils with disabilities and/or special needs from special and mainstream schools. Special school personnel could be utilised to facilitate the integration/re-integration of disabled pupils into mainstream schools as well as to provide support for mainstream pupils experiencing difficulties in learning. Joint programmes could be developed to address common curricular concerns such as transition to the adult world. Mainstream teachers could create a broader curriculum for special school pupils and modify their teaching approaches for pupils with special needs within the mainstream setting. Teacher exchanges could be arranged to facilitate the sharing of knowledge and expertise.

Developing a 'whole-school' response is crucial to the success of any integration programme. Schools that successfully educate pupils with disabilities can be distinguished by certain common characteristics (Hegarty, 1993b). What these schools share in common is a clear policy which affirms the value of all pupils. This guiding policy informs the work of all school personnel especially in their relationships with pupils. Modified teaching approaches are utilised to mediate the content and delivery of the curriculum. There are sufficient skilled staff within the school who share their expertise with their colleagues. As a result, all school personnel participate in the education of pupils with disabilities. Generally, a successful partnership between home and school has been forged which contributes to the successful education of pupils with disabilities.

Effecting change at school level can be challenging given the competing demands for resources and scarce expertise. Schools are expected to prepare pupils for adult life, maintain academic standards, expand curricula in response to a rapidly changing world and enable pupils to develop social and personal skills. As a result integrating pupils with disabilities may not be a high priority for some schools.

Professional development for school personnel and the appointment of a special needs co-ordinator/co-ordinating team may begin to facilitate a 'whole-school' response to the inclusion of pupils with disabilities within mainstream schools. Two main issues need to be addressed in relation to professional development. Teachers' perceived incompetence in dealing with pupils who have disabilities and/or special needs must be tackled. Also the attitudes of teachers, other school personnel and mainstream pupils are crucial to the success of any integration programme (Jenkinson, 1993). It is essential that all class teachers should have a working knowledge of disabilities and their educational implications. Appropriate support for some pupils with disabilities may involve relatively minor adjustments to school organisation. Initial and in-service training could ensure that all teachers have a positive orientation towards disability as well as an understanding of what can be achieved in mainstream schools (Hegarty, 1993b). Specialist training is also necessary for support personnel in mainstream schools. This type of specialist training is noticeably deficient for support personnel in post-primary schools (Lynch, 1995). To date, training has developed in an ad hoc manner frequently resulting in uneven provision and a lack of co-ordinated services.

The appointment of a special needs co-ordinator/co-ordinating team from within the teaching staff has proved effective in responding to pupils who require special educational provision (Butt, 1993).

The co-ordinator/co-ordinating team can initiate school-based strategies which:
(a) identify, assess and provide on-going support for pupils with disabilities and/or special needs who require this service.
(b) enable class teachers to take responsibility for all pupils within the class including those who have disabilities and/or special needs.
(c) assist teachers to develop appropriate educational programmes.

(d) promote positive teacher expectations for the progress of all pupils including those who have disabilities and/or special needs.

(e) develop positive attitudes to disability among mainstream pupils.

(f) ensure that pupils with disabilities and/or special needs are given access alongside their peers to 'whole-school' activities.

Conclusion

Facilitating access to mainstream schools for pupils with disabilities represents a challenge for all educators. Accepting that disabled pupils have a right to be in mainstream schools is the first step.

However, educating pupils with disabilities cannot advance in isolation. Exploring the pathways indicated in this article may help us to realise that our common task as educators is to create the welcoming school which embraces difference and values diversity. The key issue for the future of integrating pupils with disabilities is articulated by Lindqvist (UNESCO, 1994) when he stated that:

> "The challenge now is to formulate requirements of a 'school for all'. All children and young people of the world [......] have the right to education. It is not our education systems that have a right to certain types of children. It is the school system of a country that must be adjusted to meet the needs of all children".

Ainscow, M. (1989), *Special Education in Change,* London: David Fulton.

Ainscow, M and Muncey, J. (1989), *Meeting Individual Needs: Studies in Primary Education,* London: David Fulton.

Barton, L. (1996), "Sociology and disability: some emerging issues". In: L. Barton (Ed.), *Disability and Society: Emerging Issues and Insights,* pp 3-17 Harlow, Essex: Addison Wesley Longman.

Beveridge, S. (1996), "Experiences of an Integration Link Scheme: The Perspectives of Pupils with Severe Learning Difficulties and their Mainstream Peers." *British Journal of Learning Disabilities,* 24, 9-19.

Butt, N. (1993), "The S.E.N. Co-ordinator in Secondary Schools". In: J. Visser and G. Upton (Eds.), *Special Education in Britain After Warnock,* pp. 83-97, London: David Fulton.

D.E.S. (1978), *Special Educational Needs.* Report of the Committee of Enquiry into the Education of Handicapped Children and Young People (The Warnock Report). London: HMSO.

Fletcher - Campbell, F. (1994), *Still Joining Forces? A follow-up study of links between ordinary and special schools,* Slough: NFER.

Flynn, G. and Kavalczyk - McPhee, B. (1989), "A School System in Transition". In: S. Stainback, W. Stainback and M. Forest (Eds.), *Educating All Students in the Mainstream of Regular Education,* pp. 29-41, Baltimore: Paul H. Brookes.

Government of Ireland (1993), *Report of the Special Education Review Committee,* Dublin: The Stationery Office.

Government of Ireland (1996), *A Strategy for Equality: Report of the Commission on the Status of People with Disabilities,* Dublin: The Stationery Office.

Hahn, H. (1987), "Civil Rights for Disabled Americans: The Foundation of a Political Agenda". In: A. Gartner and T. Joe (Eds.), *Images of the Disabled, Disabling Images,* pp. 181-203, New York: Praeger.

Halliday, A. (1993), "Educational systems: Who Belongs?" In: P. McGinley (Ed.), *Recognising Needs and Abilities: Sharing Life With People Who Have Intellectual Disabilities,* pp.55-63, Renmore, Galway: Brothers of Charity.

Hegarty, S. (1993a), "Reviewing the literature on integration". *European Journal of Special Needs Education,* 8(3), 194-200.

Hegarty, S. (1993b), *Educating Children and Young People with Disabilities: Principles and Review of Practice.* Paris: UNESCO.

Jenkinson, J. (1993), "Integration of students with severe and multiple learning difficulties." *European Journal of Special Needs Education,* 8(3), 320-335.

Jowett S., Hegarty S. and Moses, D. (1988), *Joining Forces: A Study of Links Between Special and Ordinary Schools.* Windsor: NFER-Nelson.

Lynch, P. (1995), "Integration in Ireland: Policy and Practice." In: C. O'Hanlon (Ed.), *Inclusive Education in Europe,* pp.61-74, London: David Fulton.

McGee, P. (1990), "Country Briefing: Special Education in Ireland." *European Journal of Special Needs Education,* 5(1), 48-63.

O'Murchú, E. (1996), "What is special about Education?", *Irish Educational Studies* (15), 252-269.

The Convention Secretariat (1994), *Report on the National Education Convention.* Dublin: The National Education Convention Secretariat.

UNESCO (1994), *World Conference On Special Needs Education: Access and Quality.* Paris: UNESCO.

Walsh, P.N., Shevlin, M., O'Moore, M., de Lacey, E. and Stritch, D. (1996), "In-service training for teachers involved in link schemes: a consultative process". *British Journal of Special Education,* 23, (2), 75-79.

Westwood, P. (1995), *Commonsense Methods for Children with Special Needs* (2nd Edition). London: Routledge.

Whitaker, P. (1994), *Mainstream Students talk about integration.* British Journal of Special Education, 21(1), 13-16.

Second Level Education for Traveller Children: A Case Study

ANNE O'BRIEN

I first learned of Nan's intended enrolment in our school when, as Primary Liaison Teacher, I visited her Primary School in May. The purpose of my visit was to collect information about enrolled pupils who would transfer to second-level in September. I received a detailed account of Nan's school career from both her sixth-class teacher and her Principal. I was then introduced to the Teacher for Travellers, with whom Nan spent part of each school day. Nan was described as a strong personality, whose learning difficulties were compounded by her lack of concentration and application which prevented her from achieving more than she did.

The accumulated information presented a challenge to us, the Learning Support teachers, in Nan's chosen second-level school. Nan had been a very good attender throughout Primary school years and, unusually for children of Travellers, she was the right age for transfer. Travellers are often older finishing Primary school, due either to late entry into the Primary system or to a delay in progress because of learning difficulties or absenteeism. These two factors - attendance and age of transfer would, her Primary teachers felt, give Nan a better chance of survival in the second-level system than her predecessors had.

Nan was not the first Traveller pupil to enrol in our school. A number of Travellers had been enrolled over previous years, though never more than one per year. To put it in a national context, research has shown that in 1993, no more than one hundred children of Traveller families, aged twelve to fifteen years, were attending mainstream second-level schools out of an estimated two thousand children eligible to do so.[1]

The first Traveller I encountered in our school was Josie who stayed for two terms. Following her, Mary sat her Junior Certificate successfully and entered Senior cycle, but did not complete the first senior years. Another Mary, a bright student, dropped out half way through second year. Nan's older sister, Mary, began third year but had left by the end of September last year. Ann-Marie, who came from difficult family circumstances, lasted only three weeks in all. Our school's experience of Travellers enrolling and staying had not been positive. It must be said that the history of attendance and age of transfer was not as favourable for those other girls as it is for Nan.

The question we must ask is, are these two factors alone, attendance and age of transfer, sufficient to ensure that Nan will receive the education to which she has the same right of access as others? Or, will the long list of factors, identified by the Task Force on the Travelling Community (1995) which affects the low rate of participation by Travellers at second-level, be likely to convince Nan that she, too should become an early school leaver?[2]

Here lies the challenge. How do we, as a school, give Nan the confidence and the coping skills she needs to continue at least to Junior Certificate? Will an inappropriate curriculum and a failure to acknowledge her cultural identity ensure that Nan, too, will leave the system early? How can Nan be accommodated within our existing structures to enable her to benefit from the social and personal development available at second-level?

The answers to these questions are controversial and difficult to implement. What is required is a commitment from the Department of Education to adequately fund schools enrolling Travellers. It also requires the good-will of both management and staff in providing intercultural curricular and support mechanisms to ease the transition for Travellers from the Primary to the Second-level system.

At entry in September, Nan took the same standardised tests as all other incoming First Years. She was found to be in the bottom twenty per cent on general ability tests; to have a reading age of below eight years on a group reading test and a reading comprehension age of below six years on a diagnostic test. Her mastery of mathematical objectives was also very low.[3] She was subsequently placed in a small group of First Years who would be withdrawn for Learning Support in English and Maths. There were no resources available to provide extra time for Nan on an individual basis. This was because all the time available was already allocated to the twenty per cent or so of Junior Cycle students requiring help with learning difficulties. Nan would follow a programme of oracy, literacy and numeracy, over four periods each week in a group of eight students. This intervention took no account of her cultural disadvantage with regard to classwork and homework, and assumed that she could cope at least as well as others in her Learning Support Group. However, through liaising with Nan's Class Tutor and year-head, it soon became apparent that some extra support would have to be provided to help Nan to settle into school. She had adopted the role of class clown in her efforts to conceal her difficulties with classwork. As a result, she was quickly becoming the focus of too many disciplinary incidents. It became clear that her lack of concentration and her active search for attention was a cover for her inability to cope with the syllabi presented to her. In subjects where she could manage the content, there was little or no behaviour problem. Textbooks had been provided but she continually "forgot" to being them to class. She was making no effort to do any homework and was falling further and further behind in terms of both class work and her teachers' expectations. If Nan was to survive in the system, there would have to be some form of further intervention. Nan was clearly clinging to her own "glass ceiling"[4], responding to the deeply-ingrained lesson she had learnt about the expectations of settled people for her.

The Learning Support team, in consultation with the Pastoral Care team, decided that it would be in Nan's best interest to withdraw her from mainstream class more frequently. Joining various Learning Support groups she could either work independently on her own programme or participate in a group activity as was most appropriate. So Nan began to attend the Learning Support Room three to four periods per day. Nan had always responded quite well in the smaller group. She liked the fact that she could do the work - it wasn't "too hard". [She shows immediate frustration and loss of concentration and co-operation if a task proves too difficult}. She also appreciates the fact that her companions in the groups are struggling with learning like herself. I think she feels less different there. She turns up promptly, cheerfully and "willing to work".

I was interested in Nan's behaviour in her mainstream class. I consulted her teachers and while they have not observed any overt prejudice towards Nan in class, they would have noticed some negative responses to Nan's presence, not least the tendency of some classmates to "laugh at" Nan's antics which she uses to attract attention. Nan does not seem to have formed any particular friendship group in her class. She is friendly to all, as is her nature, but experiences the occasional rebuff from her classmates. She may, therefore, be feeling somewhat isolated within her class. Nan is unwilling to discuss this matter herself.

Following the increased intervention in Nan's mainstream education, teachers began to get a little more feedback from her. Her behaviour improved and some effort was being made by her in some subjects. An increased awareness of Nan's difficulties, background and circumstances left Nan's teachers with a more understanding and sympathetic approach to her. They expressed a strong desire to be better equipped to help pupils like Nan, who are failing in Junior cycle, because of a combination of unsuitable curricula, teaching materials and an insufficient knowledge of Traveller culture. This acknowledgement of our need and willingness to seek help open the way for the setting up of structures where pupils with difficulties like Nan's whether Travellers or not, may be able to follow a more appropriate and perhaps reduced curriculum to Junior Certificate. This demands a commitment from the Department of Education and from school management to allocate the necessary resources.

While we remain faithful to our ethos and policy of open access to our school, will Travellers continue to feel welcome to enrol? We must be prepared to learn more about their culture and to provide an appropriate curriculum for them to follow. With this in mind, we have invited the Visiting Teacher for Travellers in Second-Level Education. With the support of our principal, this in-service will take place before the end of the present school year.

All the most recent research shows that the best way to help the Travelling Community to become fuller participants in our education system is to offer an intercultural curriculum to all our students in all our schools. A wonderful opportunity exists now with the introduction of the new civic, social and education (C.S.P.E.) programme at Junior Cycle. There are options within this programme for work on intercultural studies which would help to promote an ethos of inclusiveness in our schools. The existence of resources such as the CROSSCARE programme, "Celebrating Difference"[5], various Pavee Point publications and The Blackrock Teachers' Centre publications, amongst others, offer opportunities for a cross-curricular approach to inter-cultural studies. Our Junior Cycle syllabi could only be enhanced by such content.

A second strategy to increase involvement by Travellers at second-level is the education of parents of Traveller Children. I agree with Mairin Kenny's premise that we, as teachers, must challenge Traveller reluctance to become involved in second-level education. The mistrust amongst Traveller parents of second-level schooling needs to be replaced with the conviction that "appropriate school experience will benefit their children, will give them further opportunity to explore the world, to acquire skills and a variety of linguistic/social registers which will enable them to negotiate their way in the world with competence".[6]

For Nan to succeed at school, the involvement of her parents is crucial. She needs their support. We need to know what it is they want for her. Working together we may be able to provide some meaningful learning experiences.

It was decided to ask Nan's parents to meet her tutor, year-head and Learning Support teacher. We needed to inform them of her difficulty in settling into school, of her difficulties with her work and of the programme of intervention which she is following. In turn, we needed to know what they want for her from school and whether or not they value a second-level education enough to ensure Nan's continued attendance. It should be said that Nan's attendance had continued to be good, with the exception of a period of illness and a few days absence where she found coming to school too difficult because of the effects of prejudice. She has experienced "name-calling" on the way home from school.

We had a very positive meeting with Nan's mother. She and her husband want Nan to get "all the schooling she can". They appear to have a good relationship with Nan where they can talk about how things are for her in school. The mother reminded us of the cultural difference between Nan and other students, citing the "name calling" as an example of prejudice and stating how she and her husband would not be attending parent-teacher meetings on the appointed days, as they feel that they "would not fit in". She did, however, express their willingness to meet teachers at another time, if requested to do so.

Given this support from home, it is critical that Nan be supported in School so that she can have positive learning experiences and can perform to some of her teachers' expectations. While teachers need to be sympathetic, they also need to make realistic demands on Nan, and as Mairin Kenny says, to beware of the compassion trap… "where fear of success is deep, compassion can inhibit rather than encourage achievement. Children in this situation need clear, secure and authoritative leadership to enable them to take risks, to face the future."[7]

It is with this last statement in mind that we believe that Nan's programme of intervention must be only temporary. Such frequent withdrawal runs the risk of segregating her from her class and accentuating her difference in a negative way. On the positive side, her increased attendance in Learning Support has given us the opportunity to know and understand Nan better. It has allowed us to determine her real levels of ability. It has made the provision of a varied, individualised programme of work with her a reality. It has encouraged and motivated her to read and write with a greater degree of success, using a multi-media approach. In fact, Nan's ability and proficiency in both reading and writing would appear to have been somewhat underestimated in the culturally inappropriate tests available. It is hoped that Nan will soon have the courage and the confidence to break through her "glass ceiling" and to reach for her true potential.

As time goes on, Nan seems to be happier and more at ease. She seems to be learning what is acceptable behaviour in the classroom and using her "clowning" role less as a means of attention-seeking. We must, as teachers, beware of attempting to get Nan to conform totally to our set of standards. We must not ignore the fact that she has her own set of values to validate. It is desirable that a balance is struck which will allow Nan to gain the social and personal benefits of enjoyable school years and which allows the school to offer her the skills and competencies which will feed her tentative ambitions to serve her own community and enhance her self-esteem.

Unlike the primary school system which has over the last ten years learnt to cope somehow with the increased participation by Traveller children, the second-level system is struggling to learn from their experience. As Mairin Kenny suggests in her article, we in second-level can, in hindsight "focus on what is offered in relation to Travellers in the curriculum for all children, in the welcoming, inclusive ethos of the school and in the provision of respectful, appropriate supports."[8]

Among the "appropriate supports" which might be offered would be the extension of the Visiting Teacher Service to second-level schools. Currently, the overstretched personnel in this service have a brief only for the primary school. Second-level teachers, and especially support teams, need access to the Visiting Teacher Service for transfer of information, improved parent contact, advice on resource materials and in-service training. The provision of the Home-School Liaison service in all our schools would also offer support.

To ensure that Nan receives "quality time" in Learning Support, we need more resources in the form of teaching hours for each Traveller enrolled. One-to-one tuition less frequently would be far less disruptive of her mainstream classwork than our current system of frequent withdrawal into groups. We hope, gradually, to cut back Nan's Learning Support time, to re-integrate her into her mainstream class more fully, while encouraging her to cope independently with classwork and homework.

In conclusion, I refer again to the questions posed earlier and the challenges faced by schools to encourage a greater participation by Travellers in the second-level system. No doubt, as Mairin Kenny argues, "schools could do more to empower Travellers to face the future, and Travellers could develop a wider vision of their future."[9] However, I leave the last word with the Association of Teachers of Travelling People who in their submission to the Task Force made the following demand: "It is essential for the Department of Education and other relevant agencies to invest the time, expertise and finance needed to ensure that the quality and suitability of educational provision for Irish Travellers meets their needs. In a multi-cultural society, it is also essential that the education system is intercultural and anti-racist and committed to equal opportunities for everyone. For change to be effective and far-reaching, reform must be approached in a holistic manner."[10]

1   *Report of the Task Force on the Travelling Community* July 1995 Par. 6(a) 1.2.
2   Ibid. Par. 6(a)2.
3   Standardised tests used were: AH2; Nelson Group Reading Test 9-14; Neale Analysis of Reading Ability; Drumcondra Criterion Referenced Maths Test.
4   Mairin Kenny: "Understanding What We See and Hear; Travellers and Second-Level Schooling." *GLOCKLAI: Journal of the A.T.T.P.* Vo.2.Nos. 3 + 4 Nov. 1995.
5   *Catholic Social Service Conference - an Intercultural Programme for Senior Primary Classes.* Blackrock Teacher's Centre.
6   Mairin Kenny: *GLOCKLAI* as (4) above.
7   Do.
8   Do.
9   Do.
10 *Report of Task Force,* see (1) above, Par. 2.5.5.

REMEDIAL TEACHING – PRAGMATIC ISSUES AND EVERYDAY CHALLENGES

AILEEN O'GORMAN

The remedial teacher works on the front line in the battle to educate a sizeable number of our school going population. Her task is not easy. It is one area of education where the vocation of the teacher can be seen. In this short article I propose to put before the reader a few of the pragmatic issues and everyday challenges which she encounters.

Name Calling

In the light of recent moves in education and the aspiration towards integration and acceptance of differences, the use of the word remedial should be re-examined.

Several names other than remedial teacher come to mind. Consider "special" teacher, "reading" teacher, "difficult" teacher, "disruptive" teacher or even "that" teacher. Another is the "learning support" teacher. This title, although a mouthful, accurately describes both the function and activity of this teacher; support for pupils, parents and teachers combined with active involvement in improving the learning process for particular pupils. This does not suggest miracles, but rather a group of dedicated professionals who are there to understand and help pupils to learn. This title raises everyone's self esteem and so I shall use it throughout the remainder of this article.

Numbers

For a school to have a learning support teacher who is not ex-quota is a mixed blessing. If she is to give her time to individuals or small groups of pupils then her colleagues must take on the extra burden of "making up" for the pupils she is not teaching. A staff may well think that this give and take is worth it, but can this extra burden be justified when staff are also being encouraged to become active members of participative management, which in practical terms means taking on more and more responsibility?

An ex-quota learning support teacher is in a better position, as are her colleagues. It is laid down by the Department of Education that she must have twelve hours per week teaching individuals, small groups or special classes (max. 16 pupils). It is at the discretion of management that she may/may not give more time to specialised teaching throughout the week. Why is it not possible for her full 22 hours to be given to the support of learning? If the school qualifies for the ex-quota position, then there are enough candidates to engage her full time in her specialised area. We should be utilising such experts to the full. Otherwise we are wasting resources.

Mixed Ability

Since the introduction of the Green Paper (Dept. of Education, 1992) schools throughout the country have been re-examining their philosophy and formulating their mission statement. Within most is an aspiration towards justice and recognition of the worth of the individual. This is one influence which has caused many schools to move away from streaming and replace it with mixed ability teaching. The report of C.M.R.S. (1988) *Equality in Schooling in Ireland* comes out very strongly against streaming. Research, though inconclusive, it says, has shown that the "bright" pupils will still do well in a mixed ability class while the "weaker" pupil will do better than in streaming.

Streaming is introduced very early on in a pupil's life in Ireland. At the pre-school level, the child's socio-economic status will dictate whether or not the child attends a pre-school. There are obvious disadvantages to non-attendance. Once in the primary school system, class teachers often operate a system of grouping by ability. What is this but streaming under a different name. The post primary school is more open about their streaming system but tend to excuse it by the number of points required for third level entrance.

Schools say that it is more practical to use streamed teaching. The teacher can plan materials, methodologies and challenges to stretch the higher ability pupils. But who wants to face the group of low achievers, all grouped together in one class? They already find school work difficult and are failing at it. Now the school has confirmed this and have let the whole community know it. What sort of message is this to give a teenager as she embarks on a five/six year course of study? No wonder she gives up. The educational system has given up on her long ago. We say we value each individual equally but we clearly value some more than others.

Part of the new R.S.E. programme is an attempt to open the pupil's minds to equality and justice. There is neither equality nor justice in a streamed system of teaching. We cannot continue to assign pupils to a system of education where we do not practise what we preach. We must address this issue before the pupils themselves make us account for our injustice and hypocrisy.

Teacher Role

What then is the role of the learning support teacher in a school which employs a mixed ability system of teaching? She does not spend all her time with individuals. She will group together pupils with similar problems and similar levels of ability. She will withdraw these pupils from "normal" class and give them special attention. Here lies the rub! From which class will she withdraw the pupil? If a pupil has difficulties with learning that have persisted into post primary school then that pupil is likely to be experiencing difficulties across the whole curriculum. Do you then withdraw a weak pupil from a subject class to give extra tuition in another subject? When the pupil returns to the subject from which she has been withdrawn, she is then at a further disadvantage having missed today's lesson. What usually happens is the pupil returns to the subject from which she has been withdrawn, she is then at a further disadvantage having missed today's lesson. What usually happens is the pupil is withdrawn from R.E. But the R.E. class is a very important class for learning life skills, an area of deficiency in many pupils. Although pupils will deny the relevance of R.E. at this stage of their lives, we all have a spiritual dimension to our humanity which needs to be explored and developed. The spiritual vacuum in modern society is being filled by extreme and sometimes dangerous sects. The R.E. class must not be diminished.

Why not withdraw from the subject in which the pupil is to get the extra tuition e.g. withdraw from English for extra tuition in English? This presents a new set of difficulties. Now the learning support teacher gets little opportunity to use her training, expertise and extra resources. She now has to operate within the confines of a particular syllabus.

New Elementary Junior Certificate

The new Junior Cert Elementary programme tries to answer these difficulties. The pupils who will follow this programme will be confined to approx. five subjects. This gives time during the day for extra tuition in these five basic subjects. The profiling assessment, also, means that these pupils, after only one year in the programme, will receive a certificate validated by the Department of Education. There are many advantages to the programme but the school must have sufficient numbers of such pupils to make up a full class. With the best intentions are we not back to streaming by another name? Will this become a cosmetic exercise to bring down the numbers of youngsters leaving school uncertified?

Multiple Intelligences

For many years experts have decried the summative written assessment on which the Irish system depends and efforts have been made to introduce alternatives. The pupil profile incorporated into the Elementary Junior Cert. is one such programme. Another is the portfolio system advocated by Howard Gardner.

Gardner is the guru of the Multiple Intelligences theory of education. He wrote *Frames of Mind* (Gardner, 1984) as an exploration of his theories of cognitive psychology, not as an educational methodology. The theory of multiple intelligence articulates what every teacher, especially those of younger children, have been saying for years i.e. if a child is weak in one area, then she is likely to be strong in another. It is question of finding the strengths and working from them. Gardner specifies seven areas of different intelligence and says that there may well be more. Most teachers agree with this theory but we constantly return to the same problem - how to assess each intelligence. This is where the portfolio system comes in. A child collects in her portfolio samples of her work as she progresses. It is not a collection of her "best" work, all corrected and neatly rewritten. Rather it is a collection of pieces (written, art, tapes, etc.) which show the stages of development of the child as she explores, reflects upon, experiments with ideas or materials. Teachers' comments and evaluations are also included.

The portfolio idea has great possibilities and should be pursued. But there are huge obstacles on the route, not least of which is teacher fears and prejudices. There is also the inference that portfolios are fine for weaker pupils but don't touch the written terminal exam of the high achiever. To introduce a portfolio system would require training, time and a massive public relations exercise. Teachers are reaching saturation point with the changes which have taken place recently, so proceed slowly.

Whole School Inspection

One of the recent innovations yet to be introduced is whole school inspection.

A small booklet (Dept. of Education 1996) has been sent to the schools. It suggests possible methods of inspection. It goes to great lengths to allay fears that we might follow the path of those across the water where a date set for the Ofsted visit causes knees to knock, resignations to be written and stress levels to soar. The booklet suggests that the inspection team may decide to investigate a particular area of the school e.g. the learning support department. How, then is the learning support teacher to meet this challenge?

I suggest a six step approach. Firstly, IDENTIFY the pupils who are failing or experiencing difficulties. This information will be contained in the entrance assessment and the September screening tests. The reports from the primary teachers will help too. Secondly, DIAGNOSE the particular difficulties of individual pupils. This will require individual testing. The help of the educational psychologist may be required here but can take some time to arrange and carry out. A talk with the parents always gives another insight into the pupil's way of thinking and learning. Thirdly, PLAN a programme for each pupil. The same plan may be used for pupils with similar difficulties and levels of ability. Some may require individual assistance. Set targets as part of the plan. Sometimes the targets can be arrived at in consultation with pupils. Fourthly, MONITOR progress over a period of time. Fifthly, REPLAN. Perhaps your targets were too high. Perhaps different materials or methodologies would be more appropriate. Lastly, RECORD what you are doing.

It is these records that the W.S.I. team will want to see. Many learning support teachers operate on intuition and have done a good job down through the years. In the new age of accountability, transparency, inspection and litigation intuition is not enough. We must have the records to back it up. I suggest a large filing cabinet, a customised record sheet for each pupil for each year of her school career. On a particular day each week get your records up to date. Record your thoughts, your discussions with other teachers, pupils and parents, tests used and test results, your recommendations and the follow up. Date everything.

Isolation

Isolation is one of the problems faced by the learning support teacher. here the local meetings of the learning support teachers are very important. There is a very active national association (ARTI) which organises a seminar in Dublin at the end of September each year. However, not everyone is able or allowed to attend. Learning support teachers must organise branch meetings within travelling distance of their schools. Attendance at a meeting each month would alleviate the feeling of isolation experienced by many learning support teachers. It would also keep the teacher abreast of new developments and create a forum for the dissemination of good practice.

The learning support teacher can feel isolated, not only from her colleagues in school but also neglected by those who should be her line of communication with the sources of innovation. It would help these branches if the Dept. of Education and the psychological services would pass on, as a matter of course, any documentation that is relevant, e.g. booklet on the Elementary Junior Cert.

Update

The last challenge I will refer to is that of inservice for the learning support teacher. The skills and practices of the learning support teacher need to be updated regularly. The learning support teachers in one area could be brought together for one day to inform/update them on current departmental policy. One might ask at this point does the department actually have a policy for learning support education?

The approach of the present minister to disadvantaged schools must be praised. It has allowed extra resources in the guise of part of a teacher, an exquota position or a resource teacher to be appointed where they are most needed. But why not involve the learning support teachers in the development of the department policy in regard to this vital area in education?

Conclusion

The clientele of the learning support teacher is increasing. We will be needed for a long time to come. It will take many years before we see a decrease in these numbers. Our jobs are secure. But will we be able to keep up? We are an ageing profession and, in my opinion, the pupils are getting livelier each year. I have to give my support to the principle of early retirement for teachers. In all honesty and with the best will in the world, I do not think that I will be able to deliver a quality service to my "special" pupils as I creep towards sixty-five.

Byers, R. & Rose, R. (1996) *Planning the Curriculum for Pupils with Special Educational Needs.* David Fulton Publishers, London.

C.M.R.S. (1988), *Equality in Schooling in Ireland.* Milltown Park, Dublin.

C.M.R.S. (1992), *Education and Poverty: Eliminating Disadvantage in the Primary Years,* Typeform Ltd., Dublin.

Dept. of Education (1992), *Education for a Changing World: An Introduction to the Education Green Paper.* Gov. Pub. Sales Office.

Dept. of Education (1993), *Report of the Special Education Review Committee,* Gov. Pub. Sales Office.

Dept. of Education (1995), C*harting our Education Future: White Paper in Education,* Gov. Pub. Sales Office.

Dept. of Education (1996), *Whole School Inspection; Consultative Conference.* Gov. Pub. Sales Office.

Gardner, H. (1984). *Frames of Mind.* Fontana Press, London.

Gardner, H. (1993). *Multiple Intelligences: The Theory in Practice.* Basic Books, London.

Hinson, M. & Hughes, M. (1982). *Planning Effective Progress.* Hulton NARE, Great Britain.

Lynch, K. (1992). "Intelligence, Ability and Education; Challenging Traditional Views", *Oideas,* 38, pg 134-148.

Madaus, G.F., Airasian, P.N. & Kellaghan, T. (1980). *School Effectiveness: A Reassessment of the Evidence. New York,* McGraw-Hill.

NCCA (1996). *The Junior Certificate Elementary Programme: Guidelines for Schools.* Gov. Pub. Sales Office.

The Junior Certificate
– A Parent's Perspective

PAT SEXTON

It seemed a simple enough assignment. At the December meeting of the Parents' Association I was volunteered to write a 2,5000 word article on the above subject. The deadline of mid-January seemed a long way off. Anyway, 250 words on each of the Twelve Days of Christmas would see the article completed with some words to spare. Panic has now set in. The deadline is only five days away and the pious aspirations for the Twelve Days of Christmas are now a dim memory of the distant past. I'm sure that the above scenario sounds very familiar to the students (and parents of same) who are preparing to sit the Junior and Leaving Certificate Examinations next June.

A recent survey quoted in the Labour Market Review, a bi-annual publication published by FAS, showed that almost 80% of school leavers who entered the labour market in 1993 without qualifications were unemployed one year later. This compared to almost 50% of those who completed the Junior Certificate Examination and almost 30% of those who completed the Leaving Certificate Examination.[1] It is clear that the less qualified have fewer opportunities now than in the past and this trend is likely to continue in the future with a Leaving Certificate being the minimum requirement of most employers. Consequently, wherever possible, the Junior Certificate must be seen as a means to the end and not just an end in itself. However, cognisance must also be taken of the students for whom the Junior Certificate will be the highest qualification attained by them. For these students (for a variety of reasons) this will be a magnificent achievement for which they must receive the maximum credit.

There are approximately twenty subjects in which the Junior Certificate Examination may be taken. While it is desirable that the student should have as broad a choice as possible in First Year, it should be possible to reduce the 'core' subjects for Junior Cert. to seven. Most employers don't care how many A's, B's, etc. were obtained in the Junior Certificate when interviewing prospective candidates for positions.

Some of the Language Subjects include an aural examination. The arrangement (for the Leaving Certificate examination) whereby the oral examination is taken in March/April reduces some of the pressure on the student when the written examinations start in June. Perhaps the Department could examine the possibility of also holding the aural test in March/April.

Traditionally there has been no oral or aural examination for English and I wonder what sound reason can be given for this omission. Maybe it is time that an oral/aural examination be included and I feel that a good case could also be made for the inclusion of Debating as part of the curriculum. The benefits would be at least threefold - confidence building in having to debate issues in front of one's peers, team spirit building by being included on a debating team and a honing of one's interview techniques. There is little point in obtaining a third level qualification at a university/regional technical college, and then being unable to project oneself properly at a job interview.

Stress is a word that is becoming very common nowadays particularly in relation to students. Even while attending National School, pupils are often asked 'What are you going to do when you leave school?' A generation ago this question generally referred to leaving school at 17/18 years of age and those who were lucky enough obtained employment with the Civil Service, Guards, or County Council. Only a small percentage of school leavers continued to Third Level Education. However, the introduction of 'Free' education, the expansion of university places and the establishment of Regional Technical Colleges now ensure that the majority of Leaving Certificate students face an additional two year's education, at least, in order to obtain some qualification to enable them to gain useful employment.

The points system, therefore, contributes in no small way to the pressure/stress that students in second level education suffer. This particular pressure/stress commences in First Year and will not abate until the student finds employment. Unfortunately, even in employment, people will be subjected to pressure/stress, albeit of a different nature to that felt by a student. Students may encounter stress in the early stages of entry to second level education. Some may have been used to classes of less than ten pupils in National school and they suddenly find themselves in classes where the norm is in excess of thirty students. In addition, being split up from childhood friends, freedom to spend lunchtime around the town and new teaching methods may also cause anxiety. Consequently, I feel that a major emphasis should be placed on relaxation techniques commencing in First Year. Perhaps these could be incorporated with the subjects like P.E., Civics, Religion and Games.

A common feature of the present education system is the 'Grind'. This is normally on a fee-paying one-to-one basis between teacher and student. Grinds have now become big business with specialised institutes and colleges organising week-end grinds, Christmas grinds, Easter grinds, etc. Recently a comment was made to me in relation to these latter grinds and the benefit earned by the student in obtaining additional points to gain acceptance to a particular course and/or university - will that student, without the further benefit of grinds, be capable of successfully completing the required examinations in university?

The cost of grinds make it much more difficult for the students of low-income families to compete with those students who can afford the grinds and thus grinds can contribute to widening the gap between rich and poor.

Another area of concern is the teacher/pupil ratio. The ratio in Ireland at present is in the region of 17/1 while in some of our European neighbouring countries the ratio can be as low as 7/1 (Belgium) or 9/1 (Italy). A reduction in class size may not necessarily improve the students' results but it should enable the teacher to devote more time to those students who need additional attention. In view of the declining birth rate, the numbers seeking admission to second level schools are decreasing and this scenario will present the Department of Education with what they perceive as an ideal opportunity to reduce staff numbers in schools. However, if they forego this 'statistical' right and retain the existing staff (together with replacing those who retire) the teacher/pupil ratio should reduce considerably over the next few years.

Career Guidance seems to be a hit or miss case in some schools. From the time students commence in First Year, they should be considering the career options open to them when they leave school. Consequently, if examinations in all ten subjects were held at Easter in First Year, the results obtained should enable the student to get an idea of the subjects at which he/she excelled. This would enable him/her to reduce the chosen subjects to seven for the Junior Certificate. At this stage 'serious' Career Guidance should be introduced to assist the student in focusing on a number of careers based on the subjects (and levels) being taken for the Junior Certificate. It is also vitally important at this stage that the student does not get blinkered in concentrating on only one career. Parents should not interfere too much with the career choice of the students as it is the student, and not the parent, who will be tied to that career for perhaps thirty or forty years.

In view of the major advances which have been made in the computer software industry, it is surprising that no company has yet developed a programme that will analyse each student's results, hobbies, likes, dislikes, traits, etc and suggest various career options which would be suitable to him/her. Similarly, the programme should be able to identify reasons why a particular career would not be suitable for that person.

Most of the recent Government announcements on the creation of extra jobs refer to the computer industry. However, second level students have received little exposure to computers within the Curriculum. Similarly, the Department of Education appears to have been extremely slow in developing computer studies as an examination subject.

Consideration should be given to continuous assessment during the Junior Cycle in which Junior Certificate style examinations are taken at the end of each of the three years in the cycle. The results obtained in the three examinations could be aggregated in some format or other to determine the overall result of the Junior Certificate. It might be possible to provide feedback to the students to enable them to learn from their errors.

1   Murphy, M. & Whelan, B.J., *The Economic Status of School Leavers 1992-94,* Dublin. E.S.R.I.

THE JUNIOR CYCLE OF SECOND LEVEL EDUCATION : VOICES FROM FRANCE

IMELDA BONEL-ELLIOTT

C oncern about the effectiveness of education at the junior cycle comprehensive secondary school ("collège") has been rising in recent years, both in France and internationally. In France the state plays the major role in the national education system. It lays down the curricula, supervises examinations and the awarding of diplomas. The emphasis in the constitution on liberty, equality and fraternity is echoed in educational policy. Schools are secular, free and obligatory. In 1994-1995, 3,286,419 pupils attended junior secondary schools, of whom about 80% were in publicly funded and managed schools and about 20% were in private schools (MEN 96.16). As one of the main aims of the 1989 Education Act was to bring 80% of a cohort to the level of the "baccalauréat" and 100% to at least the level of the first vocational diploma by the year 2,000, the "collège" has become a preparatory school for further education. There have been many reforms of the junior cycle in France since the early sixties, culminating in the 1996 reform. An outline of the major reforms of the junior cycle over the last thirty years and a study of the 1996 reform, of the teaching of modern languages in France and of the role of ancillary staff will provide the basis for making some constructive suggestions about policy and practice at junior cycle.

Traditionally there were three different schools and educational routes for young people in France at age 11 and selection operated mainly on lines of social class. The junior comprehensive school for all with three distinct streams was set up in 1963 (Lelièvre 1990). It was divided into two cycles: the two year observation cycle and the two year orientation[1] cycle (Robert 192). It was hoped that these reforms would lead to equality of educational opportunity but research has shown that even if there was some social mobility, selection according to school results often led to recruiting the educational elite from the social elite (Prost 1986).

The Haby Act in 1975 set up the unified junior comprehensive school with a common core curriculum. Selection and streaming were banned. With the arrival of a socialist government in 1981, a committee under the chairmanship of Louis Legrand was set up and its report was published in 1983 (Legrand 1983). It recommended a junior comprehensive school with mixed ability classes, team teaching and interdisciplinary themes. As this policy was implemented, it was often difficult for teachers to adapt to teaching pupils of very different levels in the same class. Banding proved to be fairly popular in some schools. Options became the hidden way of operating selection. Taking German as first foreign language and Latin as an option generally enabled pupils to be in a "good" class as they were reputed to be difficult languages. In order the help the "collèges" in disadvantaged areas, educational priority areas (14.2% of all "collèges) were set up in 1982 and they received extra financing including extra teaching staff (MEN 95.25).

Reforming the education system in France and providing secondary education for all in a junior comprehensive school meant creating social unity by giving everyone the same education. The comprehensive ideal was formulated on the basis of educational justice, that is, equality of opportunity via standardised schooling. The emphasis was on uniformity and standards set by a centralised government (Deroutet 1992 & 1996). The notion of providing equality of opportunity through schools was undermined by sociological research in the 1960s and 1970s which seemed to show that equality of educational opportunity was a myth (Bourdieu and Passeron 1970).

The traditional emphasis on providing the same education for all in order to achieve equality of opportunity was eroded in the late 1980s and 1990s. Other principles seemed equally valid: the notion of community and environment, efficiency, well-trained people for the needs of the economy and the market principle (Deroutet 1996). Moreover providing equality of education opportunity began to be interpreted in a different way in official circles, for example a report written and published by the famous "Ecole Nationale d'Adminstration" stated that it was necessary to identify each young person's individual level and to provide differentiated help for pupils (ENA 1989). Increasingly there was a move away from providing a single curriculum in a single school to a differentiated approach.

The 1996 reform of the junior cycle builds on the increasing emphasis since the early 1980s on decentralisation. In the period 1975-1985 there was a transition from the notion of a single school to a decentralised school with a school plan. The 1989 Education Act was a major innovation in education policy as it proposed finding local solutions to local problems with the sate as supervisor and no longer as manager of the system.

From 1996, the junior cycle is divided into three cycles: the cycle of adaptation (first year), the central cycle (second year and third year) and the orientation cycle (fourth year). The aim of the junior comprehensive school is to provide a general education for all young people who have completed primary school. The knowledge and skills imparted at the "collège" provide the basis of a common culture for the whole nation. The "collège" aims to develop each child's personality, to prepare him/her for citizenship and to help him/her to choose the educational path which will enable him/her to achieve cultural, social and vocational integration in society (B.O. 1996). Instead of providing a uniform type of education, stress is now laid on adapting the curriculum to suit the local situation and on responding to the needs, aptitudes and interests of a diverse school population. Schools are also encouraged to organise visits to companies and work experience.

Each class in first year is allocated 26 hours of teaching but the number of hours of teaching each pupil gets per week is 23-24 hours. The extra 2-3 hours can be used to provide extra help in the main subjects, French, mathematics and a modern language, for the weaker students. In order to qualify for these extra hours, volunteer teachers must formulate a proposal which must be approved by the board of management and must be incorporated into the school plan. The reform stresses local initiatives and not systematic help for all pupils in difficulty or increasing the number of hours for all. The main emphasis in the new curriculum is on literacy, numeracy and oracy for all. Thus each class has 5/6 hours of French per week and 3/4 hours of mathematics. A modern language, history, geography and civics, science, technology, art, music and physical education are all obligatory. The time devoted to each subject is set nationally. The syllabus is centrally prescriptive only in outline and leaves each school free to adapt it to local circumstances. Two hours per week of supervised homework are provided for first years and increasing emphasis is laid on providing methodological help for pupils.

Reforms in France are introduced after a series of pilot studies. Several innovations have been experimented to try to improve the performance of the disadvantaged including: individual tutoring, remedial assistance with reading, supervised study, extra teaching in some subjects in small groups, advice on study and good work habits (methodology), teaching in smaller classes, computer aided learning (Monde de l'Education, 1994). A survey of school principals would seem to show that individual tutoring, remedial assistance with reading and supervised study do help weak students (Monde de l'Education, 1994). Indeed some teachers feel that extra teaching in small groups helps disadvantaged children to feel good in class but does not radically alter the academic performance of the majority of this group.

The central cycle (second and third years, 12-14 year olds) is to be reformed in 1997. This reform emphasises parental choice and local initiatives. 25.5 hours of teaching are provided for each class to cater for the core curriculum and extra hours are provided for options. The minimum number of hours in each subject comes to 20, so each school can use the 5.5 extra hours to provide a diversified response to the needs and interests of the pupils which can include some teaching in smaller groups. Each school can organise special classes in third year with a specific curriculum provided they get official approval and provided that pupils are only assigned to this class if their parents so wish. A second modern language is obligatory for all pupils in third year. Latin is an optional extra in the central cycle. Technology or a regional language can also be taken (B.O. 1997).

Streaming with grouping of subjects will only take place in fourth year. There will be two groupings: the modern language option and the technology option. Although there is a common core curriculum, the weaker students are more likely to take the technology option. However no pupil can be assigned to this stream without the agreement of his/her parents. This is a major change in France where traditionally, class teachers assigned pupils to streams and groups of subjects.

While many teachers and principals are enthusiastic about the opportunities for innovation at school level that the reforms of the junior cycle provide, many feel that most reforms are designed by bureaucrats to try to reduce the cost of education and that the service provided for pupils has deteriorated (SNES 1997). Some feel that the emphasis on the disadvantaged is a levelling to the lowest common denominator and that the overall result is a lowering of standards as pupils receive about 23 hours instruction per week now instead of about 27 hours before the reforms. The more cynical would even go so far as to say that the emphasis on local initiatives rather than providing systematic help to all weak pupils enables the state to reduce the cost of education as many teachers do not have the time nor the expertise to write up projects in order to obtain extra funding. Moreover the most underprivileged in the worst schools with the highest staff turnover are bound to lose out as teachers who are going to move will not take the time to innovate. Thus many teachers say that lip service is being paid to the disadvantaged while at the same time the state is making cutbacks and the disadvantaged are perhaps no better off.

A positive aspect of the French core curriculum is that all young French people study a modern language for at least four years. 99.4% of all secondary pupils study at least one modern language (most for at least seven years); 70.5% of all secondary pupils study at least two modern languages (the second language for at least five years); and 10% of all secondary pupils study three modern languages (MEN 95.46). The main modern languages are English, German and Spanish but teaching is also provided in Italian, Arabic, Chinese, Hebrew, Portuguese, Russian, Dutch and Polish. Moreover 55.5% of all pupils in the last year of primary school were introduced to at least one modern language in 1994-1995 (MEN 95.47). In an era of increasing European integration and globalisation of trade, when many Irish people may have to work with people whose mother tongue is not English even if they live in Ireland and when some may want to work in countries where English is not the main language and where they may have to communicate with people of other languages, it seems increasingly important that all Irish pupils should learn at least one modern language and that at least two thirds could learn at least two modern languages. Moreover it is at least as important to learn modern languages for cultural reasons as for utilitarian ones.

In post-primary schools in France, the state provides ancillary staff so that teachers can get on with the job of teaching. To give an idea of the extent of ancillary staffing, I will give a concrete example of a "collège" in my area. This school has about 620 pupils (slightly above the average size). There are about 38 teachers, a full-time principal, a full-time assistant-principal, two administrative secretaries, a full-time educational adviser[2] (in charge of extra-curricular activities and general discipline including absences), 4 monitors (university students who supervise study and general discipline including absences), a bursar, four assistant-bursars (who also have responsibility for the canteen and the accounts of two schools), a caretaker, and a cook. I have not included the cleaning staff and the assistant cooks. This seems to be a very positive side to the French education system as teachers have time to get on with the job of teaching and to keeping their professional expertise up to date.

In conclusion, the French junior cycle is worthy of close attention. It is interesting to compare the French definition of a core curriculum with the curriculum areas defined by the NCCA (NCCA 1993). The notion of providing a common culture for all French citizens is important especially in the context of integrating immigrants. However in the secular French Republic religion is considered to be the responsibility of the family and all pupils have

Wednesday afternoons free in order to attend catechism classes. Differentiation in the curriculum only occurs around the age of thirteen/fourteen, which is about the age at which most Irish pupils have completed one or two years of secondary schooling. Would Irish people think it desirable to have a common core curriculum for the first year of post-primary education? Perhaps the results of the pilot studies on innovation to help the underprivileged might be of some interest to Irish educationists and planners.

It is important for Irish policy-makers to consult the staff of post-primary schools before making any reform and to avoid making the same mistakes as their French counterparts, that is, giving the impression that their main motive is cutting costs and not improving the system.

Irish schools need to provide more teaching in modern languages. Not only should more pupils be learning at least two modern languages but there should be a wider choice of modern languages available nationally - perhaps the proposed regional education boards could play a role in co-ordinating this new policy in each area.

Now that the religious orders are increasingly withdrawing from secondary schools, it is necessary for the schools to have more ancillary staff in order to function more efficiently. In order for Irish secondary school teachers to have the time necessary to devote to being professional experts in their domain and to teaching their pupils, it seems imperative now to provide staff for the non-teaching tasks in schools. In this way, Ireland's schools can be modernised and made more comparable to their continental counterparts.

B.O. *(Bulletin Officiel)*, No25, (20.6.1996).

B.O. *(Bulletin Officiel)*, No 5, (30.1.1997).

Bourdieu, Pierre et Passeron, Jean-Claude (1970) *La Reproduction,* Paris, Ed Minuit.

Corbett Anne and Moon, Bob. (1996) *Education in France: Continuity and Change in the Mitterrand Years* (1981-1995), London, Routledge.

Derouet, Jean-Louis. (1992) *Ecole et Justice,* Paris, Editions Métailié.

Derouet, Jean-Louis. (1996) "Lower secondary education in France: from uniformity to institutional autonomy", in Anne Corbett and Bob Moon (eds) (1996) *Education in France: Continuity and Change in the Mitterrand Years* (1981-1995), London, Routledge, pp.253-269.

Education Act (1989), "Loi d'orientation sur l'éducation", *Journal Officiel* 14.7.1989.

ENA (Ecole Nationale d'Administration). (1989) *Le système scolaire en France,* Paris, Berger-Levrauylt.

Legrand, Louis. (1983) *Pour un collège démocratique,* Paris, La Documentation

Française.

Lelièvre, Claude. (1990) *Histoire des Institutions scolaires* 1789-1989, Paris, Nathan.

MEN (Ministère de l'Education Nationale). (novembre 1995) "L'enseignement des langues vivantes étrangères à l'école primaire en 1994-1995", Note d'information DEP 95.47.

MEN (Ministère de l'Education Nationale) (1996) *Programmes de 6ème,* Paris, CNDP.

MEN (Ministère de l'Education Nationale). (mai 1995) "Les zones déducation prioritaires à rentrée 1994", Note d'information DEP 95.25.

MEN (Ministère de l'Education Nationale) (novembre 1995)"Les langues vivantes dans le second degré dans les établissements public s et privés à la rentrée 1995", Note d'information DEP 96.16.

MEN (Ministère de l'Education Nationale) (avril 1996) "Les élèves du second degré dans les établissements publics et privés à la rentrée 1995", Note d'information DEP 96.16.

MEN (Ministère de l'Education Nationale). (juillet 1996) "La fonction de conseiller d'éducation et conseiller principal d'éducation", Note d'information DEP 96.31.

Monde de l'éducation (septembre 1994).

NCCA (1993) *Curriculum and Assessment Policy towards the New Century,* Dublin, NCCA.

Prost, Antoine. (1986) *L'Enseignement s'est -il démocratisé?* Paris, PUF.

Rancurel, Marc. (1995) *Guide to Secondary Education in France,* Strasbourg, Council of Europe Press.

Robert, André. (1993) *Systéme éducatif et réformes,* Paris, Nathan.

SNES (Syndicat National des Enseignements de Second Degré). (1997) *L'US,* No 423, 8.2.1997

1   Decision-taking period. "Orientation" means choosing one's educational path and also one's career.

2   See MEN DEP 96.31 for more details.

PROMISES TO KEEP –
THE EVOLUTION OF ENGLISH AT JUNIOR CYCLE

TOM MULLINS

Recently at a meeting of English teachers in Dublin, a teacher from the west of Ireland remarked to me, "I'm doing such interesting work with my Junior Cert. students.....I'm enjoying it a great deal and they are too....you know, I actually think they find the examination a bit of an anticlimax". These comments have stayed with me because I consider them symptomatic of the success of the Junior Cert. English syllabus and of the manner that most teachers have taken it on and brought its promise to initial fruition. This, it needs be said, has been achieved by English teachers with the minimum of support by way of in-career development courses or an abundant supply of resources. It is then most appropriate to highlight the quality of this achievement and to reflect on what is the best way forward now to ensure that the syllabus remains a creative context.

To appreciate what has been achieved it is necessary to remind ourselves just how radical the syllabus was when it was introduced in 1989. That was a definitive date in the history of the subject English in this country. For the previous hundred years or so, surviving all changes in Irish society, English was based on what is commonly known as the "cultural heritage" model. The basic assumptions of that model were that all students should learn Standard English and should be initiated into reading the great literature of the past enshrined in the pantheon of authors called the canon of which Shakespeare is the "veritable Zeus". Irrespective of either social and cultural background or ability this was essentially to be the Irish student's experience of English. A colonial relic if there ever was one!

The Junior Certificate English syllabus challenged this monolithic, hegemonic view of the subject on a number of fronts. It problematised its definition of literacy by asserting the need for a variety of literacies in the domains of personal, social and cultural action; it introduced an approach to the reading of literature which was not determined solely by cultural heritage thinking or traditional academic stances. As possible elements within the subject these were not eliminated but the idea of literary experience was broadened and not seen as confined exclusively to certain texts defined by their criteria; adolescent literature was given a significant role and the media (so long seen as the cultural enemy) found a place. Students were encouraged to read widely and to generate personally meaningful interpretations of texts. Finally the traditional distinction between language and literature study was removed: the subject was to be experienced as an organic unity where all the elements interacted within integrated structures called syllabus units.

The thinking behind these innovations was that if English was to achieve its real end, fostering the personal growth of students through language, it had to reach directly into the students through language, it had to reach directly into the students' interiorities and so forge links between experiences with texts and their own feelings, needs, desires and interests. The syllabus sought to install literary experiences of a meaningful kind as the dynamic centre of the subject; from that centre everything else was to grow.

Post-modern culture with all its energising democratic variety but also with its insecurities, arising from the rejection of traditional cultural narratives, shaped the new syllabus. As such it offered a challenge to teachers' perception of their role in a number of ways. For example, the majority of teachers were trained in the traditional model of the subject and were accustomed to having certain texts selected and prescribed by the Dept. of Education. That "traditional narrative" was now stripped away. Teachers were expected to choose appropriate texts, plan coherent programmes in cooperation with colleagues and develop a range of new methodologies which would help to realise the aims and objectives of the syllabus. For many this was a daunting prospect and the source of some anxiety. Nevertheless as early as 1992 in *School Communities and Change*, a research survey on the impact of the Junior Certificate on schools carried out by the Marino Institute of Education, 80 percent of English teachers welcomed the new syllabus although about 30 per cent wished for more specification in the syllabus statement. Another survey, published privately by the Association of Teachers of English in 1993 found that the majority of teachers were most appreciate of the new freedom they had to exercise their professional responsibility but felt that they needed more advice and support in order to structure their courses. These surveys suggest how teachers quickly adapted to the aspiration and direction of the syllabus despite the challenges it offers. At this stage, in 1997, it appears that the initial unease has diminished and teachers have successfully developed a *modus operandi*. The role of the examination papers in bringing about this situation has been significant; they have reassured but at the same time have left an important space for teachers to use their initiative.

While the teacher quoted at the beginning of this article felt in some way left down by the examination (she is not alone in this opinion) it must be acknowledged that the inspectorate have in difficult circumstances consistently attempted to produce papers which reflected the spirit and orientation of the syllabus. There has been a "sea-change" in the format, approach and tone of the papers since the first examination in 1992. They are now bright, well designed, student-friendly in tone and the visuals and other texts invite the student to engage with them. In this context it is particularly appropriate to mention the success of the Foundation Level paper in serving its cohort of students. According to teachers the students, due to their ability to complete the paper, are achieving a high level of personal satisfaction which they have rarely experienced in an educational context. This together with the eventual affirmation that most students receive from their grades indicates that the introduction of the Foundation Level Paper has been a successful innovation.

However, despite these achievements there is an anomaly in having an open syllabus assessed only by a terminal written examination. The NCCA English Course Committee who designed the syllabus were aware of this and recommended that the effects of the terminal examinations could be ameliorated if such modes of assessment as an oral test and a portfolio of work could be introduced in even a limited way. For a variety of financial and logistical reasons these recommendations were found to be unacceptable. As a matter of interest the report, *School Communities and Change*, showed that a high percentage of teachers were in favour of introducing "orals, aurals and projects" into the assessment procedures. So from a theoretical perspective and from the experience in the schools the interface between the syllabus and the examination procedures is a matter of concern. It is felt that despite the best efforts of the papers to respond to the syllabus there is a great deal of interesting teaching and learning going on that is not receiving the official recognition it deserves. (Whether it needs such recognition to affirm its value is a matter of conjecture).

This is not an easy matter to resolve. If the examination and the syllabus are not successfully articulating then one or both of them have to change; either the modes of assessment must become more flexible or the syllabus must lose some aspect of its freedom. To achieve a satisfactory solution to this issue it would be advisable to set up a research project to examine what gains and losses might result from a variety of adjustments. Only after such a careful, thoughtful approach should any changes be made in the present situation. Ad hoc solutions would not be desirable.

But to return to the actual teaching of syllabus.....The most successful innovation has been the introduction of media studies. Teachers consistently report on the high level of involvement that students exhibit in the area. (Even some national newspapers have seen it as an opportunity; their motives for publishing regular media supplements may be ambiguous but ironically these ratify the social validity of this dimension of the syllabus). Teachers find that students are frequently more culturally equipped than themselves to cope with the media. It is because of student enthusiasm for the media that there is an urgent need for teachers to be given the inservice that can turn this enthusiasm to worthwhile educational ends.

At the moment, media study tends to be confined to the print media, because these are closest to traditional language study within English and are relatively easy to provide and examine. But in the immediate future it will be vital that television, film and radio are studied because it is those media more than any of the others which feed the imagination and work on the sensibilities of the students. They will need to be introduced to ways of "reading" these media which are appreciative, critical and reflective. With the imminent onset of the new Leaving Certificate English syllabus where film study is available as an option this development is most desirable.

Calling for a more inclusive media course makes it necessary to define more clearly, than has been done heretofore, the objectives of such studies within English. The stance of English should be experienced as being distinctly different from a commercial approach to the media. For example, in analysing an advertisement it would be quite inappropriate within English if the issues of the value-systems, assumptions and ideologies informing the persuasive techniques in the advertisement were not the central focus. Since

English at its core is a humanistic study it should consider cultural artifacts, here media products, with a reflective, critical stance which foregrounds the integrity and freedom of the human person and questions any attempts to undermine them. It should develop in students the capacity to see through the manipulative tendencies of the media in all their forms and equip them with the language and skills to resist their powerful voices. Such an approach would give English a much more explicit political role in our democracy than it previously had and emphasise its centrality in the curriculum in a new and significant way.

Another important achievement of the new syllabus is the profile and status it has given to the genre of "adolescent literature". Initially there was some doubt expressed about the literary quality of these texts but in general they have become acceptable. This is mainly because they can provide worthwhile literary experiences and also because they are an important source of "pedagogically appropriate material" outside of the neat "yellow-pack" selections of the commercial textbooks. They are real books that have an authentic existence outside the classroom in a way that textbooks never have. Nevertheless there is an issue that the use of these texts raises. Many teachers both in the past and present emerging from university degree courses and teacher training courses have not read widely in the genre. They are unaware of the riches that are available to them for their teaching of literature. This lack of expertise needs to be taken seriously in hand. Teacher Guidelines can be of some help but there is a need for more than that to make good this deficit in teacher training at second level.

As noted earlier, teachers had commented in the various surveys that they were uneasy about how to organise their courses within the new syllabus provision. The original proposal of using syllabus units designed in a specific manner to plan a course was not found to be amenable or indeed workable. Furthermore since those units were given no place in the assessment procedures, they soon lost any applicability except in some textbooks. It is now clear in hindsight that those syllabus units should not have been used to quantify what was to be covered by the students. However, the idea of the unit has had a lasting effect. While Junior Cycle programmes are in the main being constructed around units based on genres of literature and language, e.g. a poetry unit, a fiction unit, a letter writing unit, etc. they have retained one of the central ideas of the original unit design, i.e. the integration of literature and language studies. In other words the literature being studied and the resultant imaginative experiences are being used to provide a motivating and meaningful context for language learning and the development of language skills, e.g. writing letters to authors, debating about issues the text raised, planning alternative scenarios and so on. This marks a significant change in the methodological strategies of teachers. Indeed teachers have acknowledged as far back as 1993 that because of the reorientation of their approach they noticed that students were much more interested and willing to engage in writing assignments. The ATE survey of 1993 revealed that over 80 per cent of those surveyed attested to this.

These then are the major areas of success. However there are other areas where there is a need for reflection and evaluation on the way the syllabus is being implemented. Drama and poetry while aspiring to take on new materials and approaches have not developed as was hoped. There are manifold reasons for this, in the main, as usual, lack of suitable resources and insufficient in-service in these highly specialised and challenging fields. Nevertheless it is important that these elements of the subject which highlight the aesthetic domain of language are accorded a greater profile in English.

In the area of drama there was a strong recommendation that play scripts should be approached from a dramatic/theatrical angle and rescued from the one-dimensional reading approach which had been dominant for many years. Unfortunately within the examinations, the questions on drama have favoured in the main the traditional approach. Perhaps if the questions on drama were oriented towards the theatrical approach it might move the situation significantly forward and teachers would be encouraged and rewarded for their efforts in that regard.

With poetry (and the short story) the situation is more difficult. There is some evidence that both genres are reducing presences in the classroom. The necessary resources for these are just at the moment not available. Comprehensive textbooks for the whole three years as currently issued by the commercial publishing companies are not the most desirable educational resources. Teachers in many cases feel deskilled and trapped by them and as a result certain areas tend to be overlooked. What is needed now is a plethora of interesting anthologies of poetry and short stories (accompanied by teacher's notes if necessary) which will re-energise these areas and restore them to having an important profile. Unless this happens there is a danger that the heart of the subject will be lost and that the Junior Cert syllabus will be reduced to a predominantly functionalist model which would be a betrayal of one of its central aspirations, the development of the students' creative encounter with literature.

From this brief review it is possible to see that English is developing a new shape in schools; it is a dynamic, evolving shape and it needs to be kept that way so that it never develops the inertia which is the death knell of any subject. The policy implications of this are many: continual investment in resources, in continuing inservice provision, in ensuring the lists of texts are renewed and in revising and modifying assessment procedures. English teachers have shown by their professional approach to this syllabus what they can achieve with the minimum of support; if the proper support structures were provided then the resultant transformation of the subject would reward any such investment many times over.

Marino Institute of Education, *School, Communities and Change (1992)*
Association of Teachers of English, *A Review of the First Cycle of Junior Certificate English (1993)*. Private publication and circulation.

LANGUAGE, LITERATURE AND LITERACY

JOE COY

A re standards of literacy falling in Irish schools? If so is the new Junior Cert English syllabus a mistake or has the current Leaving Cert contributed to the malaise? Many people would accept that the philosophy behind Junior Cert English is realistic and worthy. Emphasis is placed on communication and the acquisition of oracy and literary skills. *"The development of skills in speaking and listening should play as important a role as reading and writing skills in this English programme"*. (1.3) The syllabus places literature within the context of language while at the same time appreciating its aesthetic and cultural values. *"The student should be introduced to the skills of reading, viewing and listening to a range of literary and media genre for aesthetic pleasure"*. (2.3.1.)

For many English teachers the new syllabus is a great liberation. The Inter Cert approach was stale and dated. Many of the texts were of marginal interest to young people and often had the effect of stifling, rather than encouraging, a love of literature. The Junior Cert has retained the dualism of language and literature. However, the approach to both has greatly broadened. Not only are the students to develop a sense of register but they are to be introduced to a wide range of writing styles both personal and functional. A completely new section on media studies brings both teacher and student into the electronic age. Within the traditional trinity of drama, fiction and poetry great scope is given to teachers as to what texts to teach. The compulsory element is gone: *"Teachers are free to choose the material they consider most suitable for their student's programme...Every effort should be made to choose material which will invite the students into satisfying and meaningful experiences.....((3.2)*

Many teachers have seized on this new freedom to introduce modern novels and plays as well as student-friendly poetry. It is refreshing to see students broaden their reading and study habits. Now they can begin at the beginning and travel the road with Scout Finch and Adrian Mole into the realms of more adult literature. A new day has dawned but the clouds are not far away.

The biggest obstacle to teaching the Junior Cert course is the Junior Cert exam. It has reduced English, once again, to a written subject despite the promise of the syllabus. *"Since the programme in Junior English is an integrated course...the assessment procedure....will also emphasise this interdependence". (4.1)*

A fluid course is being tested by a static exam. Even the most idealistic teacher has to keep an eye on the exam. At the end of the day the teacher is judged on one criteria only – the number of A, B and C grades. To achieve these much sought after letters, exam technique becomes all important. Success is more likely if energies are focused. Detailed knowledge of one play is more likely to get high marks than a sweeping knowledge of six. Why read and study an anthology of poetry when 6 carefully chosen poems (including 'Mid-Term Break') will do the trick? As for listening and oral skills – forget them. They are not tested or graded so therefore they are of no 'value'. The Inter Cert may be dead but its spirit lives on. The corpse has been resuscitated by some teachers and a timid Dept. of Education. Instead of pressing ahead with an oral/aural component to the new exam the Dept has postponed the implementation; of its own plan. The teacher Unions, naturally, expect their members to be paid for this extra work and school managements have concerns about the timing of these tests. Neither problem is insoluble if there was a will to do so.

The second cloud over Junior English is the present Leaving Cert. After the freedom of the Junior Cert comes the narrow restrictions of the senior cycle with its emphasis on acquired knowledge and rote learning. The soaring eagles of Junior English become the tame parrots of Leaving Cert English. It is not surprising that there is concern at falling levels of literacy – the present exam with its totally predictable exam paper ('an Irish poet will come up') is an obstacle to literacy. The teacher who seeks to go outside the confines of the prescribed course or attempts to foster creative thinking in students is seen as a bad teacher for wasting students' time. Debating is not on the course. So why waste time on it. Commercial English and Communication studies are not part of it. So why waste time on them. In fact why bother teaching when a set of magical notes from the local grind school has all the answers. So students spend hour after hour digesting useless tit-bits of information about Gaelic modes in Clarke's poetry or recurring animal images in *King Lear* as if this useless information was of any value outside Trivial Pursuits.

In his lectures on *The Idea of a University* John Henry Newman drew a sharp distinction between learning and knowledge. It is ironic to think how accurately his 1852 lectures reflect current realities:

"Education is...the preparation for knowledge and it is the imparting of knowledge in proportion to that preparation...We must be parties to the work...The practical error of the last 20 years...has been the error of distracting and enfeebling the mind by an unmeaning profusion of subjects...of considering that an acquaintance with the learned names of things and persons...was not dissipation of the mind but progress.....Knowledge is something more than a sort of passive reception of scraps and details....Wise men have lifted up their voices in vain; but at length, lest their own institutions should be outshone they have been obliged....to humour a spirit which they could not withstand and make temporising concessions at which they could not but inwardly smile".

The Junior Cert approach to English is the right one if it were fully implemented. Clearly there are problems at present. These are partly caused by some teachers who seek to revert to the old cut-and-dried methods (notes and quotes) and want a return to prescribed texts and petrified ways. The formulaic setting of the exam papers by the Dept. also allows other teachers (especially fee-per-lesson ones) to cynically promise high grades by exploiting the freedom offered by the new course.

Another factor which might explain declining levels of literacy is the perception of English as a subject. It belongs to the category of General Subjects which, it is believed, anybody can teach. Likewise class sizes don't matter. While Art and Science are limited to 24, 30 plus is seen as no problem in an English class. But this is farcical. How can speaking or writing skills be taught to a mob? How can a language be taught without constant monitoring and assessing? Essay type answers cannot be corrected on the board like a maths' problem or an account. The practical problems involved in teaching Home Economics, Art, Science, Drawing and Woodwork are recognised in class limits of 24. Why is the most important subject in education not given similar consideration?

If one accepts with Newman that the purpose of education is the training of good members of society and that *"it is education which gives a man a clear conscious view of his own opinion and judgments, a truth in developing them, and eloquence in expressing them and a force in urging them"* then the current Leaving Cert Syllabus leaves a lot to be desired.

Much of the discussion about the content of the new Senior Cycle English has centred on the texts to be used. Whatever decisions are made I hope it gives teachers the freedom, as the Junior Cert syllabus states to *"be guided by his/her knowledge of the student's general stage of development, linguistic abilities and cultural environment'.*

Learning can take place only in an environment where there is rapport between the student and the mentor and where the medium is seen to be of value to the student and of interest to the teacher. Of equal importance are modes of assessment because in the real world these determine to a greater extent what is studied. Ingenuity, imagination and greater resources are required if this problem is to be solved.

If English is seen primarily as a means of communication then the skills of communicating should take precedence. As the Junior Cert. Syllabus so eloquently puts it students should be able to listen and speak as well as read and write. The texts are not an end in themselves – they are a means to an end. Literature is the product of language and not the source of it. The literate student is the one who can think and feel, who is open to experience and has the confidence to speak with clarity and fluency; it is not the student with the super memory and narrow mind who can regurgitate other people's notes on other people's writing.

A Critique of the Theory Underpinning the Junior Certificate Course in History and the Reality for Pupils in the Classroom

James O'Donoghue

Teachers grappling to come to terms with the demands of the new Junior Certificate Course in History, need to clearly ascertain its aims. Its breadth can be off-putting and, short of a seemingly gradualist chronological development over the three-year cycle, initially confusion may reign. This essay will explore the theoretical foundations of the new Course and, having briefly considered the experience of history-teaching in Irish schools, it will evaluate the reality of the new Course for pupils. It is self-evident that the latter will be anything but definitive: its reality for pupils and teachers alike is evolving as the Course gains acceptability.

Brief comments on History in Irish schools need to be made before investigating the Junior Certificate approach. History has had a chequered, often divisive, career in Irish schools. The twin pillars of nationalism and religion loom large therein. For too long history was not a subject but a creed, not a discipline but a weapon. Rather than history having the dual functions of enabling "man to understand the society of the past and to increase his mastery over the society of the present",[1] "the 'Victorian mind' set great store in the power of teachers and school-books to mould mass mentality....This belief was widespread among....nationalists as well as loyalists".[2]

Fitzpatrick gives an account of the utilisation of history by both Irish states post-partition to consolidate their position.[3] The "Notes for Teachers" which served as guidelines in the southern State from 1926-1971 do show that both the Intermediate Certificate History Course post-1971 and, even more so, the Junior Certificate Course, represent remarkable, if belated, progressions.[4] Traditional history-teaching in Irish schools, then, has been unappealing, characterised by "shockingly low standards of instruction and class boredom" which did, at least, save pupils from "effective indoctrination within school hours".[5] There is a tremendous onus, therefore, on today's history teachers to fire their students with a love of history, balanced by care in avoiding bias or narrow selection. Perhaps this generation of teachers, availing of the Junior Certificate's foundations, can compensate for their predecessors' errors.

D.C. Watts claims that because history is a stereotype, history teachers progressively refine it "from its beginnings as a comic strip to a modest level of subtlety".[6] Berend argues that "what must be recognised is that present and past cannot be separated from each other...Present and past are mutual starting points for understanding each other".[7] This echoes Carr's perspective: he argued that "history is meaningless in a static world. History in its essence is change, movement or...progress".[8] In Ireland history has been taught as a separate subject in Intermediate Examinations only since 1903. The new Course envisages study of a vast timespan. Tosh argues that "the broader the scope of the enquiry, the greater the need for theory...which actually attempts to explain the progress or pattern in question",[9] a viewpoint I can readily agree with and one acknowledged also by the creators of the new Course.

He outlines the perceived dangers of theory-oriented history and their advocates, who stress that "theory denies not only the 'uniqueness' of the event but also the dignity of the individual and the power of human agency".[10] Even A.J.P. Taylor et al, however, admit that historians are obliged to classify people into groups to aid their syntheses, which "is not, therefore, a denial of human individuality...Theory does not devalue the individual; it seeks rather to explain the constraints which limit people's freedom and frustrates their intentions, and in doing so it uncovers patterns in history".[11] The validity of theory-oriented history must be accepted; the topic needing address, is the nature of its application to the Junior Certificate Course.

The new course may be the only thorough, professional experience of history for many students. Its potential impact is crucial. Whereas Sections II and III allow for in-depth, selective study, the overall structure is of necessity broad, focusing on patterns, the evolution of modern society etc. Marx's "periodisation" of history has obvious parallels with the new Course's tripartite nature.[12] Tosh's exposition on Marxism highlights more parallels: just as Marx attempted "to reveal the long-term structural factors which render certain historical developments inevitable in the long-run",[13] so the Junior Certificate attempts to provoke student recognition of patterns of development, of progress; to recognise like Jenkins that "history is a shifting, problematic discourse", that it is not "the facts per se but the weight, position, combination and significance they carry vis-à-vis each other in the construction of explanations that is at issue".[14] The new Course's theory is solidly based on this philosophy, focusing not only on the discrete facts "but the how and why and what these things meant and mean".[15] Just as comparative history has been useful "in sharpening our awareness of the fundamental differences between the periods or places under discussion", so also the Junior Certificate emphasis on the awareness of context and the command of sources should "ensure a proper relationship between theory and evidence".[16]

The approach to a syllabus attempting to explain the huge range of local, national and international history must avail of children's interest in the books, events, places, and personalities of historical significance. These voluntary responses - empathy with the subject and the Historical Imagination - must be developed. As Watts put it, "school history should evoke a historical response, and...develop a sense of the past"[17] While children should be encouraged to "range widely over historical material, experiencing its breadth and variety", they should also have opportunity to "encounter a limited number of topics frequently enough...to experience the deepening process...to see that the evidence has its limitations...and that there are disagreements about the conclusions we draw".[18] Thus, in Sections II and III of the new Course, in particular for the Higher Level student, the theoretical belief is that there will be a progression from simple and concrete data to the more complex, abstract and significant.

Watts believes that by the age of 13 "most children have the kind of chronological framework that they will retain as average adults", enabling historical 'sorting-out' to be achieved, albeit in a generalised manner. He concludes therefore that "there is no point in the teacher organising his work on a detailed chronological basis".[19] This theory can be recognised in Watts' advice and should be borne in mind by teachers: "a psychologically sound way...of making up a history curriculum, is to arrange episodes or topics in a sequence based sometimes on a chronology but often on some other principle, interrupted from time to time by a project more specifically chronological which unobtrusively strings many of the episodes together".[20] Though this approach makes assumptions about children's first level learning, the new Course does, rightly, move away from a narrow presentation of a limited time-frame, retains a recognisably chronological structure and evolution[21] and, as primary schooling appears to focus strongly on history, is a valid approach.

Crowley correctly applauds the element of progression in the new Course,[22] and Tosh stresses that a representative selection must be made.

Students must be made aware of the concept of progress. The slogan "From Plato to NATO" may appear glib and conceptually useless but it does indicate the extent and, arguably more importantly, the vast potential of Junior Certificate History. The formulation of the new Course was undoubtedly an attempt to "come to grips with the really significant questions in history".[23] Inevitably there will be an inclination to generalise and stereotype, in particular before in-depth studies. Nonetheless, the emphasis on sources, drawings, illustrations, model-building, activities, field-trips etc. retains validity. Though stereotyping may be condemned, stereotypes do "give a historical experience and leave them [students] better-equipped to deepen it [historical experience] next time".[24]

As alluded to earlier, the reality for pupils is constantly evolving as the new Course gradually gains appreciation. The one constant problem I encountered, however, when researching the reality of the new course was the time constraint. Callan argues convincingly that its accommodation within existing timetables would be a determining factor for its success or failure".[25] My own, limited, 'coal-face' experience has been considerably soured by having just two class a week in one school (three in my present school) to implement my methodology, to give the "inspirational talk followed by a vigorous discussion".[26] Too often I find myself returning to the textbook to ensure progress. The reality of school-day intrusions - school games, retreats, musicals, etc. - further erode away precious time. In this respect, Departmental guidelines on timetabling, suggesting that history should receive a 'block' of classes could prove beneficial. As one exasperated teacher succinctly put it, "I would love to indulge in the gamut of Course activities but in two classes a week I'm required to cover a thousand pages of textbook"! No doubt his frustration is accentuated by the knowledge that some of his peers have the relative luxury of three classes a week. There is a fundamental flaw in the system here.

It must be admitted that the utopian 'perfect syllabus' is unattainable. However, does the new Course achieve its aim of catering for the whole ability range without inviting "classification of students into ordinary and higher level classes?"[27] In general, this has been broadly achieved though, I fear, for negative reasons. At one level human laziness is a factor but, more pressing, is the admission by teachers that they have retained the teaching methods from the Intermediate Certificate. They assume all students are doing the Higher Course and therefore do not stream their classes. Thus, while to the Department's gratification streaming is not apparently occurring, the negative motivations for this are implicitly critical of the Department which has failed to provide adequate teacher retraining. It is the student who is suffering from this omission. Consequently, the benefits of the Course are unconsciously weighted in favour of the high achiever to the detriment of the weaker pupil who may struggle in non-streamed situations. This fundamental weakness needs to be addressed.

The teaching of the new Course must be geared towards the examination. Examination requirements need to be clear and unambiguous. Unfortunately some confusion arose over the study of special topics. Question 6D(b) 1993 upset many students when, having followed Departmental guidelines to study 'The Rise of the Superpowers or Moves towards European Unity or African and Asian Nationalism' they discovered that only two of the three topics were examined! Such simple flaws undermine the whole Course, undeservedly, as the examinations have generally proven popular and fair. Their breadth and variety have pleased teachers, ensuring a wide choice for students and an examination of many skills as well as knowledge. However, the perception that almost no student can fail the examination is having a negative impact. The Course's reputation is being undermined by this patently absurd notion. Students are not impressed by a no-fail subject because, when they come to decide on Leaving Certificate options, History may be dismissed as unchallenging. For any subject, low failure rates are a reality: history should be no different.

Under the Cycle's time constraint certain important elements, not specifically outlined in the official guidelines, but which a teacher may identify as imperative, must be forfeited. Watts explains that in Britain many students fail to gain any understanding of eighteenth-century history.[28] Unfortunately, and erroneously, this also holds true in Ireland and proves to be a major loss for the pupil and a major weakness of the Course. The theory of the new Course is progressive. Yet the reality is that it has a major structural failing. It imitates traditional interpretations, in both Irish historiography and Irish education, of the period 1691-1778 as being relatively unimportant. Crowley correctly emphasises the 'usefulness' of history in helping us to know ourselves.[29] As Callan explains, one new aim of the Course is to "understand the contemporary world through the study of the past".[30] It strikes me as incongruous that some of the decades most critical for an understanding of the contemporary Irish situation remain ignored. The student has been deprived of the opportunity of an indepth study of the only Irish battle that held European centre-stage (Boyne); of the massive (and influential) eighteenth-century Irish diaspora, particularly to continental Europe; of the Penal era; of the emergence of a distinctive Ulster society and economy. In future syllabus revisions I would hope that the Williamite [and Cromwellian] Confiscations could suffice as the 'Plantation' option for higher students.

Students must be inspired. Yet in the vitally important first school year at secondary school the pupils are confined to Ancient and Medieval History. While the Celts, Greeks and Romans etc. are important subsections for any History Course, the reality is that students are generally more interested in Modern History. There is an obvious difficulty in balancing breadth and depth. I would suggest that the university model wherein the history student enjoys each year the opportunity of studying Ancient, Medieval and Modern History, Irish and World, in an attractive mix, is perhaps preferable to the current Junior Certificate system. The heavy emphasis on Greece/Rome is outdated. The Vikings and the Normans, crucial influences in Ireland, are covered/examined in far less detail. Simply put, to grab First Years' attention and interest, I believe a modern history section, even just visual presentations, is important if the teacher wishes to retain the students' interest.

The attempt to vary the presentations of History is laudable and welcomed by pupils. Analysis of the historian's skills and difficulties is important. My own students were glad to see errors pointed out to them about our textbooks, as it showed that history is constantly changing and being revised.[31] Though there are a lot of pious aspirations regarding field trips, special activities, local history work etc., these are often impractical and expensive. In this regard, it is interesting to note the observations of two older history teachers. They both admit to having a preference for the Intermediate Certificate Course which was narrower, more detailed and, they believe, had more time for specialised work.[32] The Department hopes that provisions will be made for a History Research Assignment....[becoming]....an integral part of the course".[33] Despite the danger of subjective marking, and from the benefit of my own Intermediate Certificate experience, I think it is crucial to have History-Project work as part of the overall grading, especially when the new Course is so activity-orientated.

The aims of the Junior Certificate History Course are broad. Problems have emerged. The overall structure of the three-year cycle may, as suggested here, need revision. Time remains a pressing problem in the classroom. But the new Course has helped to revive Junior-Level History. Its theory is solid, certain practical aspects need assessment, but students are realising the vitality, the relevance and the importance of History for them. Thomson wrote that the historian "must seek to make the process of change intelligible...apply...certain techniques of analysis, exploration, interpretation....to elicit...some better understanding of how these things [history] came to pass".[34] If Junior Certificate students gain at least some of these techniques, if history's entertainment value[35] is realised, perhaps it will never again be said that ignorance of history "drives them [children] very often into evil associations, and combinations!"[36]

1 E.H. Carr, *What is History?* (London 1961; 1982 edn) 49.

2 David Fitzgerald, "The Futility of History: A Failed Experiment in Irish Education" in Ciaran Brady (ed), *Ideology and the Historians* (Dublin 1991) 168. As Fitzpatrick explains, "the concepts of 'scientific' and impartial history had few Irish exponents". ibid. 169. For the exploitation of Irish history for the purposes of nationalism by the Irish Christian Brothers, see the work of the Australian academic, Barry Coldrey, *Faith and Fatherland: The Christian Brothers and the Development of Irish Nationalism,* 1838-1921 (Dublin 1988).

3 Interestingly the number of senior students in Northern Ireland taking history decreased from 86.4% in 1922 to 37.1% in 1931. Fitzpatrick, op cit 176 n.39.

4 These notes make for disquieting reading. Fitzpatrick gives a flavour: "Teachers were further advised to tolerate 'no distortion of the facts of history nor any deliberate suppression of facts derogatory to national pride. Irish history has been much distorted by those who wrote from the enemy's standpoint". ibid. 176-7.

5 ibid. 183.

6 D.C. Watts, *The Learning of History* (London 1973) 91.

7 Ivan Berend, "History as a Scholarly Discipline and 'Magistra Vitae' in Brady (ed), 195.

8 Carr, op cit. 126.

9 John Tosh, *The Pursuit of History* (London 1984; 1992 edn) 183.

10 Tosh refers to the distinguished British historian A.J.P. Taylor informing his audience that the only lesson taught by the study of the past is the incoherence and unpredictability of human affairs"! ibid. 158.

11 ibid. 161.

12 Tosh emphasises Marx's opposition to "rigid periodisation" while also admitting that sole focus on the forces of production excludes race, religion, nationality, and is therefore a serious flaw. ibid. 166-7.177.

13 ibid. 168.

14 Keith Jenkins, *Re-Thinking History* (London 1991) 27,33.

15 ibid. 32-33.

16 Tosh, op cit. 182-183.

17 Watts, op.cit. 82.

18 ibid. 83.

19 ibid. 89.

20 ibid. 90.

21 What Crowley calls "a broadly chronological framework". Niamh Crowley, "The History Syllabus" in Tony Crooks (ed), *The Changing Curriculum* (Dublin 1990) 111.

22 ibid. 110.

23 Tosh, op cit. 182-3.

24 Watts, op cit. 92.

25 He also makes valid arguments for increased resources and more in-service training. Pat Allan, "A Teacher's Perspective" in Crooks (ed) 121. These demands do not appear to have been met and, consequently, the Course's potential can not be fully realised. A number of teachers have suggested that double-periods are essential for the more detailed activities planned. Austin makes a similar point. Roger Austin, "An External Perspective", in Crooks (ed) 125.

26 Watts, op cit. 96.

27 Crowley, op cit 107. The Department's own guidelines read: "Only in the last section....is a clear distinction made in the amount of material to be studied by Ordinary and Higher Level students.....Care has been taken therefore to ensure that the new syllabus does not demand streaming if such did not prevail heretofore". Department of Education, *The Junior Certificate: History - Guidelines for Teachers* (n.d.) 3.

28 Watts, op cit. 88.

29 Crowley, op cit 115.

30 Callan, op cit 117.

31 Brockie and Walsh, following O Corrain, wrongly claimed that the first Viking attack on Ireland happened in 795 at Lambay Island. It was, in fact, on Rathlin Island, 791.

32 They do acknowledge that this may just be unwillingness on their part to change.

33 Department of Education, op cit. 21.

34 David Thomson, *Europe Since Napoleon* (London 1957; 1981 edn) ii.

35 "A ...obvious use of history is that it is entertaining...a social gain not to be belittled". Berend, op cit 197. He quotes Bloch to support this view.

36 Rev. John McMenamin of Stranorlar, Co. Donegal, to the Powis Commission. Quoted in Fitzpatrick, op cit 172 n.21.

HISTORY AND CULTURAL HERITAGE IN THE CURRICULUM

KENNETH MILNE

It was only to be expected that both of the new political jurisdictions that emerged from the government of Ireland Act of 1920 and the Anglo-Irish Treaty of 1921 would see education as a vital agent in nurturing commitment to Northern Ireland or the Irish Free State, as the case might be. And in no area of the curriculum was this more obvious than in the teaching of history. Nor was there any abnormality in this, for school history was seen throughout Europe as having a patriotic, indeed moral, purpose.

In the twenty-six counties the subject was viewed quite explicitly as an agent for the promotion of the Gaelic ideal, and many of the founding fathers of the quasi-independent Irish state believed that an Ireland free, but not Gaelic, would only be half a loaf. They hastened to put in place measures that would compensate for what they considered, with some justice, to have been former policies that had paid scant attention to things Irish, and had, at best, neglected the Gaelic-nationalist strand in Irish life. From now on the language was to hold a position of primacy in Irish life and in the Irish educational system.

The teaching of history was to be a means to that end. The first minister for education was the historian, Eoin Mac Néill, who said: "I think that ignorance of Irish history is the chief cause of want of interest in the Irish language".

The Protestant minority in the Free State, despite the crucial role played by Protestants in the language revival movement, was, for the most part, indifferent to the welfare of the language. With the new state policy, they experienced what would probably now be termed "cultural aggression", to the extent even that student teachers were required to use (sometimes invent) Irish language forms of their personal names, and infant classes, whatever the language of the home, were to be taught totally through the medium of Irish. The efforts made by the leaders of the Church of Ireland to resist what they regarded as the imposition of an unfamiliar culture on their children are well-documented, but were unavailing. For, while the state wished no harm to their religious tradition - being willing, for instance, to facilitate the use of history text-books especially commissioned by the Church of Ireland - where the language was concerned there were no concessions, other than those made necessary be sheer practicality.

It is not my brief in this paper to discuss matters in Northern Ireland. Suffice it to say that there the situation was rendered very different, for, by a paradox, the educational system of the south gave Protestants no let out from the rigours of state policy, especially where the language was concerned, while the *de facto* denominational system of the north ensured that in the teaching of Irish and of Irish history the Catholic community (at, of course, great financial cost to itself) could to a large extent, follow its own inclinations.

It has been the common perception of people in the south that Irish history was scarcely taught in the 'state' schools of the north, other than in a British context, and contact with many northerners has led me to believe such to have been the case. With curriculum developments in the teaching of history in the north, especially at primary level, local and by definition Irish history came increasingly into the picture, but for all that, a situation developed whereby in our respective systems, north and south, we were educating children for divergence.

In recent decades, an awareness has developed in both jurisdictions that this was happening; the most serious element in the situation being that there was not only a divergence between two states, but between two traditions within one state. Hence, I presume, the northern programme of Education for Mutual Understanding, which it is not my place to say more about.

In what had come to be the Republic, consciousness of the significance of history teaching in the current Irish political situation surfaced gradually, though attempts to address the issue have not been as explicit as in the north. Doubtless this is partly the case because there has not been the same gulf between the religious communities here, such gulf as does exist being gradually narrowed as society in the Republic moved in a more pluralist direction with which the Protestant population feels increasingly comfortable, and in the achieving of which it believes that it has played a part. I think I could go so far as to say that modern generations of Protestants here see no conflict between their religious commitment, loyalty to the state, and love of their country. I should add that our concept of diversity has to embrace more than differing religious traditions, though the religious/political division is one of the more significant.

Recognising that, inevitably, Irish history has been seen by many as largely one of conquest, colonisation and rebellion, the story of a community, such as my own, whose destiny appears totally to have been bound up with an Established Church that was the ecclesiastical wing of the British state, takes a bit of coming to terms with. Recent generations of Protestants have been encouraged to do so. Understanding history enables us take account of the European dimension, and of how very differently the state was understood in times past, and that to apply the norms of parliamentary democracy and religious freedom to ages when things were perceived very differently, is simply bad history. Similarly, developing a more historical approach to the teaching of Irish history is bound to have implications, for instance, for the view that the creation of Northern Ireland is a mere short-lived aberration from a supposedly inevitable course of events.

We do not have a specific programme here in the Republic for EMU-Education for Mutual Understanding. But we do have a government White Paper entitled, appropriately, *Charting our education future.* Much of the White Paper is being subjected to close scrutiny. Not a great deal of attention has, however, been paid to one phrase: (p10) which speaks of the importance of fostering an understanding and critical appreciation of the values - moral, spiritual, religious, social and cultural, which have been distinctive in shaping Irish society. The question surely arises: what do we mean by Irish? And the White paper designates these values as those which have traditionally been accorded respect in Irish society. At this point I ought to make it clear that, as I understand it, the point being made is not that pupils should be led away from the values with which they have grown up, rather that they should be encouraged to examine these values more closely. Pupils may well come from a tradition that the school wishes to foster, indeed may be expected by parents, to foster. As in true ecumenism, you need to know your own position, and even be confident in it, before you reach out to those of other persuasions. The White Paper encourages us to take that further step.

I began by illustrating how state policy here has traditionally had a place for the teaching of history, history taught with a specific political purpose that today we might wish to broaden. But the answer is not to seek to achieve some kind of remedial action by similarly doctrinaire approach, which may scarcely do justice to present day understanding of why history is in the classroom. It is, however, no distortion of the purpose of history, rather the reverse, if we use it to create insight and understanding in political matters. In the school situation, the capacity for empathy is also, nowadays, included among the valuable historical skills. So that, to put it simply, those who empathise with the horrors of the Siege of Derry also become aware that similar endurance was called for in Limerick a few years later, and vice-versa.

Events such as Derry and Limerick have entered into our folk-memory, which, like our individual memory, can be faulty and selective. We do not seek to erase it, but perhaps we can the better inform it, and this is no easy task when folk-memory, the more bitter the better, can be turned to narrow political use. Nor should the difficulties we face in Ireland be naively glossed over. For it is not easy to commend one tradition to another in a political situation at the centre of which is the question of who is to exercise power. Yet Irish culture, and by Ireland I mean the island of Ireland, is a more variegated thing than is often recognised, however much political, dare one say, sectarian baggage it carries. Could it be the task of the school curriculum to help us to jettison the baggage? Easier said than done! But, while I can only speak of what is being done in this jurisdiction, perhaps it will become clear that at least a start has been made.

At primary level, where a radical revision of the curriculum is underway, history is part of a group of subjects known by one of the various acronyms that we are learning to live with these days : Social, Environmental and Scientific Education (SESE). In this context, history is seen as more than the agreed (or, indeed, disputed) story of the past, but as a living field of enquiry, something that has evidence, and interpretation of that evidence. Children will be encouraged to look at the diversity of cultures and traditions throughout Ireland, Europe and the world, and encouraged to empathise with people very different from themselves.

But SESE is more than history : there is geography, and there is science. Here again, and in areas such as Social, Personal and Health Education (SPHE), attention will be paid to values, diversity, human inter-dependence and citizenship. This is not to say that pupils are to be nurtured in some kind of cultural esperanto. Rather, we should bear in mind, to misquote an English writer, "How shall they know Ireland, who only Ireland know?

At post-primary level, we can detect certain echoes of the primary approach, especially in the Junior Certificate history course, and in the form of -another acronym - CPSE, or Civic, Social and Political Education, aiming to enable pupils to give reasons for holding particular views, and to be able to change their minds in the light of new evidence. And at senior cycle the history syllabus, now undergoing a process of careful revision, is also expected to place emphasis on the development of critical and analytical skills.

In other words, while much of the knowledge-base of the curriculum, however updated, is of the same species as previous generations encountered, there is an attempt, not only to identify connections, but also to engage the pupil's mind in such a manner as to educate as well as inform.

In conclusion, perhaps I should try to forestall the legitimate criticisms of those who might say that talking of the skills of the historian at pupil level, particularly where the primary school is concerned, is unrealistic, even pretentious. But some of us would claim that at the very least, such an approach will help to familiarise pupils with the need to find out what lies behind the statements in the text-book, and with experience, begin to form judgements for themselves. Some people reading this have worked much more closely with syllabus revision than I have, and I am sure that they could explain much better than I can the processes that I have merely sketched.

Those of us involved in curriculum work in the Republic are conscious that we must have a keen sense of responsibility to our society. I think that we are also increasingly aware that much that we do may have implications beyond our borders. We would like to think that our sense of responsibility is sufficiently comprehensive to take account of that fact.

LANGUAGE TEACHING AT
JUNIOR CYCLE

CATHERINE FITZPATRICK

Foreign language teaching is an important aspect of the Junior Certificate curriculum. From the outset the N.C.C.A.expressed a concern that all students should undertake "adequate study of a modern European language," (Guide to the Junior Certificate 1989). The focus is on modern European languages because of the European Union context:

"Ireland's membership of the European Union serves as a backdrop to the Junior Certificate and provides a wider context for its implementation."

The desirability of all students having access to a modern European language was reiterated by the N.C.C.A.in Curriculum and Assessment Policy Towards the New Century. (1993):

"All pupils should have access to the study of a modern European language and it is expected that the great majority of pupils would take such a course to examination level."

The modern languages offered for the Junior Certificate Programme are French, German, Spanish and Italian. All schools offer at least one modern language and many offer two.

Why Study Modern Languages?

The increasing importance of modern languages in the Curriculum has been widely acknowledged in recent years in the context of political and economic developments in Europe and the rest of the world. The economic and vocational benefits emerge as an important motivational factor in the study of foreign languages as was confirmed in the National Survey on Languages, 1993 (I.T.E). However, we must remember that languages also fulfil the general aim of education as stated in the Guide to the Junior Certificate '89:-

"To contribute towards the development of all aspects of the individual , including aesthetic, creative, critical , cultural, emotional, intellectual, moral, physical, political, social and spiritual development, for personal and family life, for living in the community and for leisure."

The specific aims of modern languages teaching are outlined in The Report of the Board of Studies for Languages '87. They are:-

- To interest and involve the learner and thus to develop in him or her the desire, capacity and confidence to use the target language(s) receptively and productively for purposes of communication at a level appropriate to his or her stage of development and ability.
- To develop in the learner insight into and openness to the culture/civilisation of the target language community.
- To develop in the learner an understanding of the specific and shared elements in cultural experiences and thus a more objective perspective on aspects of his or her own culture/civilisation.
- In association with other areas of the language curriculum, to develop in the learner a critical awareness of language as a system of communication.
- To develop in the learner the capacity to understand and respond appropriately to a variety of spoken and written material in the target language.
- To develop in the learner the capacity for creativity and imaginative self-expression in the target language(s) at a level appropriate to his/her ability.
- To give the learner a positive and enjoyable language-learning experience that will encourage and facilitate further language learning.
- To develop in the learner the desire and confidence to establish and maintain contact with members of the target community.
- To enlarge the learners options in work, further education and leisure.

Participation Levels

The study of foreign languages is not compulsory for the Junior Certificate. However, participation rates have increased steadily over the years and are now relatively high. In 1994, 1995 and 1996 over 70% of Junior Certificate students studied a modern European language.

It is of concern, however, that almost 30% of students do not study a modern language. Effectively this means that many students are denied an important area of experience in language learning. They may also be limiting their future educational and employment prospects. Research reveals that there is a high degree of variability in the extent to which foreign languages are offered by schools and studied by students. Ruane in her research on Access to Foreign Languages in Second Level Schools ('90) concluded that uneven curricular

provision, allocation and choice patterns in foreign languages are denying many students the opportunity of studying foreign languages. She examined three important variables which determine participation rates in subjects:
- Provision
- Allocation
- Choice

Provision

Provision in languages is not distributed equally throughout the school system. There are clear distinctions in the types of schools which are likely to offer them to students. In the majority of cases secondary schools are the best providers of modern European languages. Community and Comprehensive Schools are the next best providers, except in German, where their provision is proportionally better than that of secondary schools. Vocational schools have significantly lower provision rates in all four languages. Geographical location was also found to be a significant variable in provision. French provision is high all over the country. The highest provision in German is in cities and large towns while provision on the Eastern seaboard and in the South tends to be higher than in the Midlands and Northwest. Provision in Spanish and Italian is equally poor in urban and rural areas.

Allocation

Provision in foreign languages does not necessarily ensure access for all students. Schools vary in the ways in which they allocate foreign languages to students. In the Junior Cycle foreign languages are allocated in one of the following ways:-
- compulsory (core) for all pupils
- compulsory (core) for some pupils
- optional, i.e. a free choice for all pupils
- optional, i.e. a free choice for some pupils
- combination system (offered as a compulsory plus optional subjects)
- rotationally, i.e. 'taster' courses with the foreign language along with other subjects offered to all students for a set number of weeks in the school year.

French tends to be essentially a compulsory subject, other languages tending to have the status of optional subjects. Offering languages rotationally is questionable, I believe students may not know after a few weeks whether they like a subject or have an aptitude for it. Also students often have preconceived notions about subjects before they enter the second-level system and many have already decided on their choice before they 'taste' the subject. From a teaching point of view 'taster courses' necessitate less time being allocated to the language in First Year. Consequently teachers are under pressure to cover a three year syllabus in two or two and half years.

Choice

Provision and allocation factors are reflected in take-up patterns. Ruane's research confirmed that ability and gender are two important criteria used to control access to foreign languages. In some schools it is assumed that foreign language learning is difficult for the "lower ability" student, that particular languages are more suited to "more/less able" students, that for certain students languages should be a core activity, that languages are a more appropriate area of study for girls than for boys and that certain pupils should have the option of studying two languages.Timetabling practices in schools can militate against students choosing a language or choosing two languages. Since languages tend to compete with each other for curriculum space, increasing provision in the number of languages offered will not necessarily result in more students choosing two languages if they are timetabled opposite each other. Similarly, uptake of languages among boys is unlikely to increase if languages are timetabled opposite traditionally 'male' subjects like metalwork or mechanical drawing. (Hannan, Breen et al '83)

Should the Study of Foreign Languages be Core or Optional?

The study of foreign languages in the Junior Cycle is optional unlike in most other European countries where the study of a foreign language has or is becoming compulsory (Eurydice Task Force '92). Consideration should be given to the inclusion of a modern European language as a compulsory area of study for all Junior Cycle students. It is unacceptable that 30% of students at this level do not study a foreign language. These students are effectively precluded from taking a foreign language in Senior Cycle and they leave school without having acquired basic skills in language learning. This situation could be remedied by making the study of a foreign language compulsory. I do not subscribe to the view that some students lack the ability to study a foreign language. The syllabuses in modern languages were designed to cater for differences in the abilities and aptitudes of young people. Also, there is certification at two levels, Ordinary and Higher. All students can achieve at a level appropriate to their aptitude and ability.

Diversification

Participation rates across the four languages at Junior Cycle reveal considerable imbalances (Ruane '90). French has traditionally been the most popular foreign language and continues to have the highest participation rates. The numbers taking German have steadily increased over the last ten years. However, participation rates for Spanish and Italian remain very low.

Policy aimed at diversification should aim to increase provision in the four languages so that all students have a genuine choice. Such a policy should include:-

- Targeting sectors to promote languages where there is low provision in particular languages.
- Improved teacher allocation to facilitate schools introducing a second modern language. (i.e. part-time hours over the quota)
- Funding for provision of equipment and teaching materials.
- Timetabling practices aimed at promoting increased participation levels.
- Promotion of a greater public awareness of the benefits of studying each of the foreign languages. Thus choices can be made in the full knowledge of the vocational and educational value of the subject.

Diversification also raise questions about the range of languages offered in schools. Since economic and vocational factors are cited as important reasons for studying foreign languages some would suggest that the curriculum should offer languages such as Russian, Japanese, Arabic, etc. I do not believe that the Junior Certificate Curriculum should be expanded to include other languages. One of the aims of the Junior Certificate is to:-

" Prepare the young person for the responsibilities of citizenship in the national context and in the context of the wider European Community."

(Guide to the Junior Certificate '89)

In this context modern European languages should be prioritised and resources should be directed at improving provision and participation rates in the subjects currently offered. Consideration could be given to the introduction of other languages at Senior Cycle through ab initio programmes or short modules. A further argument against introducing other languages at Junior Cycle is the problem of "curriculum overload". Subjects like technology and computer studies have been introduced to the Junior Certificate programme and in some schools this has been at the expense of foreign languages. Any further expansion of the curriculum is likely to impinge further on language provision.

Syllabus

There is a common syllabus framework for the four modern European languages. The syllabus is common for Ordinary and Higher level students and thus facilitaties mixed-ability teaching. Differentiation between Higher and Ordinary level students occurs at the assessment stage. The syllabus aims to develop the four basic language skills of listening, speaking, reading and writing. These skills are taught in an integrated manner. The syllabus adopts a communicative approach with an emphasis on the use of the target language in the classroom. While the communicative approach has been very successful in promoting listening and reading skills, concern has been expressed concerning writing skills. Accuracy is a problem here. This would suggest that more attention should be given to grammar teaching to make pupils aware of languages as a system of communication.The desirability of exposing students to communicative grammar teaching from an early stage in the Junior Cycle has become increasingly obvious in the context of the syllabus. Course Committees have expressed the view that there should be a common approach to language awareness across all the languages in the curriculum. The majority of students study Irish, English and a European language so there must be considerable overlap in grammar teaching. If all the languages adopted a common approach and used common terminology students would benefit as basic language concepts would be reinforced. The N.C.C.A. should provide a forum so that the various language Course Committees can discuss a common approach to language awareness.

Assessment

Assessment across the four languages has been standardised.

The skills assessed are:
- Listening Comprehension.
- Reading Comprehension.
- Written Production.
- Oral Production (optional).

The relative weighting of the four components is similar in all the languages. Problematic areas for assessment are:
- Oral Production
- Listening Comprehension.

Oral Production:

Oral assessment is currently optional. Consequently only a minority of students are assessed. Course committees are of the view that the absence of an oral exam militates against the implementation of the syllabus aims and objectives. It can also have an undesirabe "backwash effect" in the classroom militating against the amount of oral activity taking place.

Listening Comprehension:

Course committees believe that the use of a common tape to examine both Ordinary and Higher levels is unsatisfactory. Differentiation is achieved on the basis of questions asked and it has been argued that more help can be given to Ordinary level students either in the directions or questions. However, there is a strong feeling among teachers that Ordinary level students would benefit from having a separate tape where the range of texts chosen would be suitable to their level.

Issues that impinge on Language Teaching:

Class size:

The average class size for languages is 30. This number militates against effective teaching of a syllabus which requires a lot of interaction with students and necessitates the use of pair work and group work activities. There is a consensus among language teachers that languages should be given the same status as practical subjects and class size reduced accordingly (i.e. Max of 24).

Time allocation:

There is concern that in some schools teachers are not getting a sufficient time allocation to teach languages. This has arisen because new subjects have been introduced to the curriculum at the expense of languages. Course committees have stipulated that 4*40 minutes periods per week are required for the teaching of languages. However, this is an N.C.C.A. recommendation and there is no departmental ruling to enforce it. Perhaps it is time to introduce such a regulation to ensure that the time allocation stipulated by Course Committees is adhered to.

Teachers Workload:

Teaching the new language syllabuses has made considerable demands on teachers both within and outside of the classroom. The teacher's workload has effectively increased. Teachers no longer rely on one text book but design their own teaching materials using authentic resource materials. Preparation of these materials is time consuming involving reading, preparation of work sheets and photocopying. Video and listening material also has to be prepared in advance as well as ensuring that the relevant technology is available and ready for use. There is a consensus among teachers that class contact hours should be reduced in recognition of this increased workload. This would facilitate teachers having time during the school day to prepare teaching materials.

Inservice Training:

Teachers need to have regular access to inservice courses to update their skills and familiarise themselves with new methodologies. Areas which should be prioritised for inservice include:-
• Grammar Awareness.
• Mixed-ability teaching.

I have already dealt with the need to promote grammar awareness at Junior Cycle level. Inservice courses on how this might best be achieved would be very beneficial. Mixed-ability grouping is now the norm in an increasing number of schools. Many teachers find the transition from streaming to mixed ability teaching difficult and they would benefit from inservice focused on teaching strategies to maximise learning for all students.

Conclusion:

The introduction of the Junior Certificate has resulted in many positive developments in language teaching. This is evidenced in the common syllabus framework, standardisation of assessment, and improved standards in terms of proficiency in reading, listening and oral skills. However, there are issues which need to be addressed such as equality of access for all pupils to a modern language, diversification, and increased participation rates. Such issues are unlikely to be addressed in the absence of a national policy on languages. The White Paper on Education, *Charting our Education Future* emphasises that all students should have access to the study of a modern European language. Now is the time to formulate a policy to realise this aspiration.

Ruane, M. *Access to Foreign Languages in Second Level Schools,* Dublin : Royal Irish Academy, 1990.

National Council for Curriculum and Assessment, *Curriculum Assessment Policy. Towards the New Century,* Dublin : N.C.C.A.,1989

N.C.C.A., *Guide to the Junior Certificate,* Dublin : N.C.C.A., 1989

Institíuid Teangeolaíocht Eireann, *National Survey on Languages : Preliminary Report,* Dublin : I.T.E. ,1993.

N.C.C.A.,*Report of the Board of Studies for Languages,* Dublin : N.C.C.A.,1987

Hannan, Breen et al, *Schooling and Sex Roles;Sex Differences in Subject Provision and Student Choice in Irish Post-Primary Schools,* Dublin : E.R.S.I., 1983

Eurydice, *The Teaching of Modern Languages in Primary and Secondary Education in the European Community* - Brussels Eurydice Task Force:Human Resources, Education,Training, Youth of the Commission of the European Communities, 1992.

Dept. of Education, *White Paper on Education:Charting our Education Future,* Dublin : Stationery Office,1995

AN TEASTAS SÓISEARACH: FORBAIRT SHUNTASACH I dTEAGASC NA GAEILGE SNA NÓCHAIDÍ

MÍCHEÁL Ó BRÁDAIGH M.A.

Tá cúrsa Gaeilge an Teastais Shóisearaigh ina ochtú bliain anois in iarbhunscoileanna na tíre. Tá mórchuid sa chúrsa seo atá le moladh. Am Tráthúil é seo chun féachaint ar a bhfuil sa chúrsa seo agus ar a oiriúnaí is atá sé do dhaltaí na nóchaidí.

Cúlra:
Nuair a bunaíodh an coiste cúrsa Gaeilge don Teastas Sóisearach leag an tAire Oideachais mar chúram air siollabas a dhréachtadh a dhéanfadh freastal cuí ar dhaltaí na nóchaidí agus ina dhiaidh. San obair seo bhain an coiste úsaáid as na tuiscintí nua a bhí ag lucht múinte teangacha de bharr a raibh de thaighde agus de dhul chun cinn déanta ag teangeolaithe le tamall de bhlianta anuas. Roimhe seo bhí siollabais nua curtha ar fáil sna nua theangacha agus ba léir go raibh dul chun cinn suntasach á dhéanamh ag scoláirí sna hábhair sin.

Bhí eiseamláirí maithe sna siollabais sin agus bhí go leor a bhí le foghlaim maidir le modhanna múinte teanga. Níor leor lomaithris, áfach. Thug an coiste aird ar an difríocht shuntasach atá ann idir an Ghaeilge agus teangacha eile an churaclaim maidir lena thábhachtaí atá an Ghaeilge do Mhuintir na hÉireann agus maidir leis an ionad speisialta atá aici sa chóras oideachais. Sa chomhthéacs seo ní miste a chur san áireamh:

- go bhfuil an Ghaeilge ina hábhar dualgais ag gach dalta (taobh amuigh de bheagán cásanna eisceachtúla).
- tá sí a múineadh sna scoileanna náisiúnta.
- tá labhairt na Gaeilge ar a toil ag páistí Gaeltachta agus ag roinnt páistí ó cheantair taobh amuigh den Ghaeltacht.
- bíonn oideachas bunscoile trí mheán na Gaeilge faighte ag roinnt páisté sula dtéann siad isteach san iarbhunscoil agus ar an láimh eile tá a thosaíonn san iarbhunscoil agus gan ach eolas an-easnamhach acu ar an dteanga.

Na Leibhéil:
Toisc an réimse leathan cumais seo beartaíodh ar thrí leibhéal a bheith ann don

Ghaeilge sa Teastas Sóisearach, mar atá Bonnleibhéal, Gnáthleibhéal agus Ardleibhéal. Ag an mBonnleibhéal sealbhaítear eilimintí bunúsacha na teanga, go háirithe nithe a chuireann ar chumas an fhoghlaimeora comharthaí a aithint, fógraí a thuiscint agus cuntas bunúsach a chur le chéile. Tá níos mó béime ag an leibhéal seo ar an ngabhchumas seachas ar ghinchumas. Ag an nGnáthleibhéal leagtar béim ar tú féin a chur in iúl go soiléir simplí. Níl aon riachtamas litríochta ag Bonnleibhéal ná ag Gnáthleibhéal cé go bhfuil sé mar nós ag a lán múinteoirí dán nó scéal a úsáid mar áis chun an teanga atá foghlamtha a bhuanú. Tá an nós seo le moladh. Tá deis sa chúrsa seo ar ndóigh amhráin Ghaeilge a shaothrú de réir mar is cuí. Cé gurb iad na scileanna céanna atá i gceist ag an Ardleibhéal, bítear ag súil le líofacht i bhfad níos mó sa chaint agus sa scríobh. Ag an leibhéal seo chomh maith déantar saothrú ar phrós de chineálacha éagsúla agus ar fhilíocht. Cúrsa oscailte ar fad é seo agus níl aon teorainn leis an méid is féidir a dhéanamh ag an Ardleibhéal ó thaobh na litríochta de.

Déantar cúram ag gach leibhéal de na ceithre scileanna teanga, mar atá labhairt, cluastuiscint, léamhthuiscint agus scríobh.

Labhairt na Teanga
Is é príomhaidhm an chúrsa ná daltaí a oiliúint i dtreo is go mbeidh siad in ann an teanga a labhairt agus a úsáid go nádúrtha mar chuid den ghnáthshaol. Tá an-bhéim sa chúrsa seo ar an gcumarsáid agus táthar ag súil go mbeadh daltaí in ann Gaeilge a thuiscint i suíomhanna réadúla sa saol laethúil, mar shampla ar raidió, ar an teilifís nó dá mbeidís ag maireachtáil i gcomhluadar arb í an Ghaeilge an teanga laethúil. An bhfuil an aidhm seo insroichte nó réadúil? Caithfimid cuimhneamh go maireann formhór mór dár ndaltaí i saol an Bhéarla. Dá bhrí sin chun a bheith réadúil faoin aidhm seo, séard atá i gceist ná go mbeadh na daoine óga seo in ann labhairt faoina saol agus faoina suimeanna féin i ngnáthchaint laethúil. Tá dealramh na simplíochta ar an méid seo ach i ndáiríre is é seo an ghné is réabhlóidí ar fad de chúrsa Gaeilge an Teastais Shóisearaigh. Do mhúinteoirí a mhúin an sean chúrsa ba gheall le instealladh é an Teastas Sóisearach. é sin ráite, is cúis mhór frustrachais dúinn mar mhúinteoirí nach bhfuil Béaltriail i bhfeidhm fós sa scrúdú seo. Cé go bhfuil na structúir don triail seo ann (creidiúint don Roinn Oideachais) níl an chuid is tábhachtaí den chúrsa á tástáil i slí córasach. Léiriú eile é seo ar phrionsabail an oideachais ag géilleadh don mhaorlathas!

Is nós seanbhunaithe é i bhformhór na scoileanna an Ghaeilge a úsáid chomh minic agus is féidir mar ghnáthmheán teagaisc agus cumarsáide sa rang Gaeilge. Tá an nós seo ag teacht go hiomlán le haidhmeanna an tsiollabais.

An Chluastuiscint:
I siollabas an Teastais Shóisearaigh aithnítear gur scil ar leith í an chluastuiscint ar gá cúram ar leith a dhéanamh di. Tá sé tábhachtach go mbeadh taithí ag daltaí

ar bheith ag éisteacht le cainteoirí eile seachas a múinteoir féin, fiú amháin más cainteoir dúchais é/í siúd. Is minic a tharlaíonn sé nach n-éiríonn le daltaí gnáthchaint na Gaeltachta, nó cláracha, teilifíse nó raidió a thuiscint. Is mór an lagmhisneach a chuireann sé seo ar an bhfoghlaimeoir, go háirithe má's duine é/í atá ag obair go dícheallach ar scoil.

Tá sé cruthaithe ag foghlaimeoirí agus ag múinteoirí na nuatheangacha i scoileanna na tíre seo gur féidir an-dhul chun cinn a dhéanamh maidir le máistreacht a fháil ar scil seo na cluastuisceana. Is mór an misneach agus an sásamh a thugann sé seo don bhfoghlaimeoir, go háirith don dalta lag ar fearr a éiríonn leis/leí, de ghnáth, sa chluastuiscint ná i ngné ar bith eile den teanga. Is athrú mór chun feabhais i múineadh na Gaeilge é an Chluastuiscint. Cloistear go rialta (sa rangtheagasc agus sa scrúdú) cainteoirí maithe líofa ag labhairt i nGaeilge faoi chúrsaí laethúla. Saibhriú breise is ea na canúintí sa chomhthéacs seo.

An Léitheoireacht:
I réimse na léitheoireachta thug an Teastas Sóisearach roinnt mhaith athruithe ar an bhfód. Cuireadh deireadh le cúrsa dualgais léitheoireachta. Fágann san go bhfuil saoirse anois ag múinteoirí an t-ábhar léitheoireachta dá ndaltaí a roghnú. Tá ar chumas na múinteoirí anois freastal ar riachtanais a ndaltaí féin agus cúrsaí áitiúla agus nithe eile ar suim leis na daltaí iad a chur san áireamh agus an t-ábhar léitheoireachta á roghnú acu. Toisc an réimse leathan cumais i measc na ndaltaí tá réimse leathan cineálacha léitheoireachta á shaothrú sa Teastas Sóisearach, mar atá, fógraí poiblí, comharthaí, foirmeacha iarratais, fógraí scoile, sleachta simplí, altanna i stíl iriseoireachta, litriocht nua-aimseartha idir phrós agus fhilíocht. Ag gach leibhéal is é an múinteoir a dhéanann an t-ábhar léitheoireachta a roghnú.

Maidir leis na leibhéil ar fad tá sé den tábhacht go bhfuil an léitheoireacht ar fad a dhéantar chomh gaolmhar agus is féidir leis an sort léitheoireachta a dhéanann daoine de ghnáth lasmuigh den scoil ar mhaithe le heolas a fháil agus ar mhaithe le pléisiúr. Tá sé mar sprioc i gcónaí go méadódh ar dhúil na ndaltaí sa léitheoireacht de réir mar a mhéadódh ar a gcumas.

An Scríbhneoireachts:
Sa siollabas seo leagtar síos na cineálacha ceachtanna scríbhneoireachta atá le saothrú ag na grúpaí difriúla. I gcás an Bhonn leibhéil agus an ghnáthleibhéil tugtar tú áite do thascanna praicticiúla - an sort scríbhneoireachta is coitianta againn ar fad, mar shampla, nóta gearr a scríobh, teachtaireacht teileafóin a bhreacadh síos, fógra simplí a chuirfeá in airde sa scoil (i.e. faoi chluiche/ceolchoirm). Bheifí ag súil go mbeadh lucht an Gháthleibhéil in ann litreacha gearra a scríobh. Ag an Ardleibhéal tá an méid sin ar fad le saothrú mar aon le haistí agus cuntais. Thar rud ar bith eile ba cheart go mbeadh ar chumas na ndaltaí a mianta féin a chur in iúl i scríbhinn ar bhealach atá oiriúnach dá n-aois.

Topaicí agus Feidhmeanna

Tá an cúrsa teanga bunaithe ar thopaicí agus ar fheidhmeanna teanga . Tá an dá ghné seo fite fuaite le chéile. Tá 29 d'fheidhmeanna teanga luaite i siollabas an Teastais Shóisearaigh (lch. 18). Bíonn na feidhmeanna céanna in úsáid arís agus arís eile i gcomhthéacsanna éagsúla. Tá cuid mhór múinteoirí tar éis a fháil amach faoin am seo gurb é an nascadh sa teagasc idir topaicí agus feidhmeanna an modh oibre is éifeachtaí. Dhealródh sé go bhfuil lucht scríofa téacsleabhar den tuairim chéanna.

Feasacht Teanga agus Cultúir :

Os rud é go bhfuil dhá theanga ar a laghad ag gach dalta iarbhunscoile níor cheart an deis a chailliúint chun feasacht teanga a chothú. Is é atá i gceist anseo ná go ndíreofaí aird na ndaltaí ar an nGaeilge ina dtimpeallacht agus ar phátrúin spéisiúla laistigh den teanga. Mar sin bheifí ag súil go ndéanfaí na daltaí a ullmhú chun na cosúlachtaí agus na difríochtaí atá idir an Ghaeilge agus an Béarla a thabhairt faoi deara. Tabharfaidh sé seo bunús maith dóibh i bhfoghlaim teangacha eile.

Baineann an Ghaeilge leis an gcultúr Gaelach agus cabhraíonn taithí agus tuiscint ar ghnéithe den chultúr - beannachtaí, amhráin, scéalta, rincí, cluichí, logainmneacha srl. - leis na daltaí teagmháil níos dlúithe a dhéanamh leis an gcultúr sin.

Tá sé den tábhacht chomh maith go dtuigfeadh daltaí go bhfuil an Ghaeilge oiriúnach do shaol na haoise seo agus don ilghnéitheacht chultúrtha a bhaineann le saol na hÉireann sa 20ú haois. Tá mar aidhm ag siollabas an Teastais Shóisearaigh go n-aithneofaí an ról atá ag an nGaeilge féinmheas a chothú i ngach dalta agus chomh maith leis sin meas ar chultúir eile.

Ceist an Leanúnachais :

Bhí ceannródaíocht i gceist i gcás an tsiollabais seo sa mhéid is gurbh é seo an leasú ba thúisce a rinneadh. Caithfear cuimhneamh, áfach, go bhfuil dhá réimse eile a bhaineann go dluth le teagasc na Gaeilge i.e. An Bhunscoil agus An Ardteistiméireacht.

Maidir leis an Ardteistiméireacht, is ábhar mór sásaimh dúinn mar mhúinteoirí gur leagadh an-bhéim ar ghné seo an leanúnachais i ndréachtadh siollabas nua na hArdteistiméireachta a scrúdófar den chéad uair i 1997. Cúis imní do roinnt múinteoirí é nach bhfuil aon teagmháil déanta ag cuid mhór daltaí le litríocht sa Teastas Sóisearach, rud a fhágann faoi mhíbhuntáiste iad i ngort na hArdteistiméireachta. Dhéanfaí láidriú suntasach ar leanúnachas dá dtosófaí ar Bhéaltriail a chur i bhfeidhm sa Teastas Sóisearach.

Tuar dóchais chomh maith is ea na hathruithe atá ag teacht i bhfeidhm i gcuraclam na bunscoile maidir leis an nGaeilge. Is léir go bhfuil gá fós le fóram a bheith ann inar féidir le múinteoirí de gach leibhéal teacht le chéile cun pleanáil a dhéanamh agus leanúnachas a chothú agus a chinntiú i dteagasc na Gaeilge ó rang na naíonán go dtí rang na hArdteistiméireachta.

CIVIC, SOCIAL AND POLITICAL EDUCATION IN THE JUNIOR CYCLE CURRICULUM.

MICHAEL STOKES

One of the aims of the Junior Certificate programme is to prepare young people for the responsibilities of citizenship in the national context and in the context of the wider European and global communities. Some of the syllabi for the Junior Certificate have a considerable civic, social and political dimension. However, the National Council for Curriculum and Assessment has been conscious of the need to develop more specific curricular approaches to the preparation of young people for their role as citizens.[1] As a consequence it has drawn up the new Civic, Social and Political Education programme.

According to the White Paper on Education 1995, each school will be expected to provided students with experience in the following areas, as recommended by the NCCA:

Language and Literature, Mathematical Studies, Science and Technology, Civic, Social and Political Education, Arts Education, Religious Education, Guidance, Counselling and Pastoral Care, Physical Education, Health Education including Personal and Social Development, Relationships and Sexuality Education.[2]

The NCCA Discussion Paper - Civic Social and Political Education - points out that it is a narrow and inappropriate view of civic, social and political education to perceive it as a single subject discipline.

C.S.P.E. embodies a core content as well as inter-disciplinary or cross curricular dimensions. The NCCA envisages that on completion of their compulsory schooling, students' understanding and experience of civic, social and political education will have been constructed from a single subject, from other subjects and from aspects of whole-school life. In other words their learning should mirror the integrated occurrence of civic, social and political phenomena in society and life.[3]

Active learning must form an important part of any civic, social and political education programme. Active learning can be defined as learning methods where students are given the opportunity to actively engage with the subject, issue or material at hand, through discussion, research activities, action projects etc., under the guidance of teachers. Active learning provides the most appropriate vehicle for the attainment of the types of objectives relevant to civic, social and political education and for the consequent development of active citizens.

How can C.S.P.E. as an area of education with "cross-curricular" applications be provided for? The term "cross-curricular" is one which often raises in the minds of teachers, principals and other educationalists the spectres of complex curricular planning. There are several ways that cross-curricular work in the area of civic, social and political education can be provided for.

For example, in History, syllabus topics such as "our roots in Ancient Civilisations" and "Political Change: Revolutionary Movements" present obvious potential for a concerted focus on the idea of citizenship, and the development of democracy respectively. In Geography, study of "Economic Inequality" provides almost limitless potential for study, at the national and global levels, of key concepts of civic, social and political education such as those of interdependence and development.[4]

The former Junior Cycle Civics syllabus contained a lot of good material but it became outdated and did not develop to keep pace with a changing world. In practice, the implementation of Civics in the classroom emphasised teaching about citizenship in a predominantly national context and concentrated on the accumulation of knowledge about specific topics, structures and institutions. The material was not very stimulating. There has been only a limited emphasis on active, participatory citizenship, the common practice being to teach about civic responsibility and citizenship rather than to educate for and through citizenship.[5]

During the mid 1980's and before the introduction of the Junior Certificate, the Curriculum and Examinations Board published a discussion paper on Civic Social and Political Studies. However, the need for specific treatment of civic, social and political education to reflect the aims of the Junior Certificate was not addressed until the early 1990s.

In 1990, the NCCA established a course committee for Civic, Social and Political Education. In 1993 a pilot programme in Civic, Social and Political Education was introduced into a number of schools.

Two hundred and eighty four new schools took up the programme in 1996.

All post primary schools will have to offer C.S.P.E. to their first year students starting from 1997.

The C.S.P.E. programme aims to -

* make pupils aware of the civic, social and political dimensions of their lives and the importance of active, participative citizens to the life of the state and all people;
* encourage and develop the practical skills which enable pupils to engage in active, participatory social interaction, and to adopt responsible roles as individual, family member, citizen, worker, consumer, and member of various communities within a democratic society;
* develop the autonomous potential of pupils as socially literate independent and self confident young people;
* encourage pupils to apply positive attitudes, imagination and empathy in learning about, and encountering, other people and cultures;
* enable pupils to develop their critical and moral faculties in agreement with a system of values based in human rights and social responsibilities;
* develop knowledge and understanding of processes taking place at all levels of society which lead to social, political and economic decision-making.[6]

The C.S.P.E. course should be timetabled for approximately 70 hours over a three year period - about one 40 minute class period per week. The content of the course incorporates four units of study.

Unit 1:   The Individual and Citizenship
Unit 2:   The Community
Unit 3:   The State - Ireland
Unit 4:   Ireland and the World.

Exemplar materials on the above units of study have been issued to post primary schools by the Department of Education. The sequence of the four units of study is developmental, taking individual pupils as its starting point and then exploring their citizenship in the contexts of the communities in which they participate, their nation and the wider world.[7]

As well as exploring the four units referred to above, students should undertake at least two individual or group action projects. An action project is one where the students are actively involved in developing an issue or topic which has arisen in class.

Civic, Social and Political Education will be examined in two modes. Students will do a written terminal examination on an answer booklet. They will also present a Report on an Action Project or alternatively will present a Course Work Assessment Book. The Action Project Report or Course Work Assessment Book can be assessed by the students' own teacher or alternatively it can be prepared in advance and submitted with the terminal examination. 40% of the marks will be allocated for the written terminal examination of one and a half hours and 60% for the Action Project Report or the Course Work Assessment Book. The examination will be at a single level.

It remains to be seen whether the C.S.P.E. programme can be more successful than its predecessor the Civics programme. One of the problems is the lack of a fully trained population of C.S.P.E. teachers. This can be addressed by inservice education and the provision of diploma courses in C.S.P.E. by the Education Departments in our third level colleges. If school managements give it a low level of priority on the school timetable it will face problems. Many schools have overloaded timetables with some students doing ten or eleven Junior Certificate subjects. The fact that the subject is being examined at a single level has given rise to a considerable amount of debate. Some teachers see difficulties with this for the less able students and other teachers feel that the more able students may not find it sufficiently challenging. To date there is no commitment from the Department of Education to introduce C.S.P.E. as a Leaving Certificate subject. All the other Junior Certificate examination subjects continue through to Leaving Certificate.

The last thirty years have seen a remarkable transformation in Irish society. The sense of national self-confidence and vitality has been strengthened by membership of the European Union and by economic progress. However drug abuse, crime and violence have increased. Respect for key institutions like the Catholic Church and political parties has declined. Traditional family and community values have become diluted as Irish lifestyles have changed enormously. Many of the changes have been positive but many reflect the loosening of old bonds and the decay of traditional standards and of shared expectations and understandings. For these reasons, I believe that the introduction of a new course in Civic, Social and Political Education is both timely and necessary.

1   National Council for Curriculum and Assessment (N.C.C.A.) *Discussion Paper - Civic Social and Political Education at Post-primary Level,* p.3.
2   White Paper -*Charting our Education Future* - pp.48-9.
3   N.C.C.A. *Discussion Paper,* p.15.
4   N.C.C.A. *Discussion Paper,* p.19.
5   N.C.C.A. *Discussion Paper,* p.9.
6   *Civic, Social and Political Education Syllabus,* p.7.
7   *Civic, Social and Political Education Syllabus,* p.4.

PHYSICAL EDUCATION IN THE JUNIOR CYCLE

DENIS O'BOYLE

*A**n opportunity now presents itself to improve beyond recognition, the physical education provision for future generations of Irish Children. This opportunity must be seized without hesitation.* (NCCA Physical Education Interim Report, 1996)

Physical Education in Ireland is at a critical stage in the development of the subject at all levels in education. At Junior Cycle, some observers would argue that Physical Education is losing its fight for survival in the already overcrowded curriculum. Ever decreasing time on the timetable given to their subject, the existence of poor and inadequate resources and facilities, a lack of qualified personnel in schools, and a syllabus which is largely ignored by most physical education teachers, all suggest that the future may be just as difficult as the past.

However, on the other hand, one can say that there are signs that all of these issues can be addressed and hopefully rectified. The most positive development can be seen in the work of the NCCA Course Committee for Physical Education at Post Primary Level, established in 1994. Furthermore, it is interesting to note that at last, the politicians appear to have recognised the value of the subject in schools. This is evident from Fianna Fail's discussion document on *Taking the lead - a Policy for Sport & Leisure* (1997), and the recently published strategic plan for sport in Ireland by the current Government, namely *Targeting Sporting Change in Ireland* (1997), which has recognised the need to "significantly increase the value and emphasis on physical education and sport at second level with a view to providing an appropriate balance for students".

This is indeed both an exciting and important time for Physical Education at Junior Cycle. This article is as much for those with little or no involvement in the subject, as it is for the Physical Education specialist, in its attempt to consider the controversial issues facing the subject at Junior Cycle in the light of the many developments that are currently taking place.

Physical Education Defined

Our starting point is one which provides us with a working definition of what Physical Education is all about. The Interim Report by the Post Primary Committee on Physical Education presented to the NCCA Council on February 1996, provided the following definition by Jewett and Bain, (1985),

"The Physical Education curriculum is that portion of the planned educational environment that relates to human movement, knowledge, understandings and skills".

It is largely agreed by most Physical Educationalists that the subject at Junior Cycle should provide a series of learning experiences designed to contribute in a holistic way to individual and collective well-being. In so doing it would involve acquisition of knowledge, concepts, technical mastery and attitudes that characterise physical education, together with recognition of its potential for integration with other curriculum areas.

However, these aspirations for Physical Education at Junior Cycle, while most desirable, are not always practical to implement.

The Provision for Physical Education in Ireland is the worst in Europe

Accordingly to Dr. Richard Fisher (1995), a member of the Executive board of European Physical Education Association, and of the International Council for Health, Physical Education, Recreation, Sport and Dance (Europe):

"The Provision for Physical Education in Ireland was the worst in Europe. Of the 48 European States, from the Atlantic to the Urals, Ireland is the only one which does not have compulsory Physical Education, and this is contrary to the principle of 'No Education without Physical Education', enshrined in the E.U.P.E.A. Declaration of Madrid, 27th October 1991".

Physical Education is not a "core" subject in Ireland, as it is in other European countries and as a result it has not always received parity of esteem with other subjects on the timetable. The White Paper on Education (1995) appears to offer little hope for any change from its current position in the Junior Cycle curriculum.

Teacher Allocation

It is estimated that there are approximately 800 Physical Education teachers in post-primary schools nation-wide, with about 50% of all schools having one.

Deenihan (1991), found that there was one Physical Education teacher to every 534 students, which also ranks very low in the comparative tables of our European counterparts. Furthermore, in regard to teacher training, the current supply of 35 specialist Physical Education teachers from the University of Limerick each year, is unlikely to meet future demands, especially if the subject becomes certifiable at Junior Cycle.

Time Allocation

The figures produced in a recent study conducted by Landsdowne Market Research (1996) for the ASTI has found that of a total of 365 replies, 80% of second level schools provide at least two class periods for Junior Cycle Physical Education for First Years, 73% for Second Years, 62% for third years and an alarming 42% for sixth year students, (Figure 1).

FIGURE 1

A.S.T.I. Teachers Survey 1996

SCHOOL YEARS PHYSICAL EDUCATION PROVIDED FOR 2+ CLASS PERIODS PER WEEK

(Base: All Second level schools)

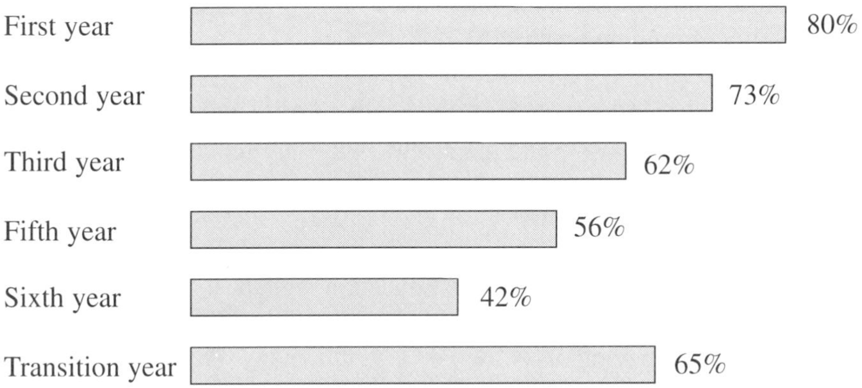

Year	Percentage
First year	80%
Second year	73%
Third year	62%
Fifth year	56%
Sixth year	42%
Transition year	65%

ASTI Teachers Survey by Landsdowne Market Research (1996)
This survey concurs with studies by Darmody (1989) and Deenihan (1991) in highlighting the disturbing trend in the reduction in Physical Education involvement as students progress through school.

The NCCA Interim Report states that the average time allocated to Physical Education in Ireland is approximately 45 minutes per week. Of 21 countries surveyed by the European Union of Physical Education the average time allocation for the subject was 2.5 times the Irish average.

It is apparent that the pressure to achieve those much sought after grades at Junior Cycle is squeezing the life out of the subject, marginalising it to the point where it has already become virtually non-existent in the time-table of a large number of schools. It has been argued that any attempt to halt this ever increasing slide, will necessitate the introduction of certification in the subject, at least to give it parity of esteem with other subjects on the Junior Certificate Curriculum, an issue we will refer to in detail later.

Facilities - The Ideal Situation
The recommended facilities as laid out in official syllabus for Physical Education and published by the Department of Education in "Rules and Programmes for Post Primary Education", states that ideally such facilities should include:

- Suitable Indoor Space: The provision of a changing and showering area should be regarded as a priority
- Suitable Outdoor Play Areas: Outdoor physical education activities require a number of suitable play areas.
- Access to Swimming pool:
- Outdoor Pursuits:
- Other Facilities: Access to classrooms, laboratories and audio visual equipment will be necessary at various stages through the programme.

Current Provision of Facilities
Regrettably, the reality on the ground bears little resemblance to the ideal as given above, in the Department of Education syllabus. Given the non-compulsory nature of Physical Education, it seems to be regarded by many as a luxury item, not paying its way. As a result many Physical Education Departments are operating on the whim of the Board of Management or Principal within the school, resulting in a negligible (if any) budget.

Furthermore, it is also important to note that for many years the provision of adequate Physical Education facilities was not a priority when the Department of Education Building Unit approved the development of school buildings.

Deenihan (1991), found that out of a total of 492 schools, 130 had no indoor facilities whatsoever, not even a large classroom. Thirty eight schools did not have any outdoor facilities and 25 schools were without either indoor or outdoor facilities.

The PEAI Members Survey carried out in 1993, showed no great improvement, and indicated that 30% of the 199 teachers who replied, did not even have the use of an indoor hall to teach their Physical Education programme.

Higgins (1992) in his survey on "Attitudes of Irish Post - Primary Principals to Physical Education" found that of the 187 Principals who replied, only 50% of the schools had a proper indoor Sports Hall, while 20% of these had no indoor hall on the school site.

Delivery of Syllabus is Restricted

According to Higgins (1992), Physical Education is, nevertheless, well resourced with outdoor facilities i.e. Tarmac areas and Playing fields, however, it is not so well endowed with indoor sports halls. This imbalance is a direct result of the large capital expenditure required to build and maintain indoor facilities. But given the uncertainty of the Irish climate outdoor facilities are often both inadequate and inappropriate, making an Indoor facility essential for the realisation of a balanced Physical Education programme for all the students in our schools.

The consequence of inadequate facilities is reinforced by the findings from yet another survey carried out by O'Boyle, D. and Ryan, E. (1994) of 74 Physical Education teachers who attended Inservice Training in ASTI House. 72.2% of them replied that they did not follow the current syllabus in the subject, as the content of their Physical Education Programme was restricted due to the lack of basic facilities and resources, and that the inevitable losers in all of this were the students.

However, this need to update the syllabus is recognised by the Department of Education and the Irish Sports Council, in the recently published Strategic Plan, Targeting Sporting Change in Ireland (1997), with a proposal to:

"Revise the second level school syllabus and implement it with an initial pilot project which would include PE/sports links as part of the brief."

Certification in Physical Education at Junior Cycle

In a survey on the Attitudes to Certification at Junior Cycle, Darmody and Halbert (1995), found that 54.3% were in favour with 39.7% against.

FIGURE 2

**Attitudes to Certification
of P.E. at Junior Cycle level**
(Darmody, M. and Halbert, J. 1995)

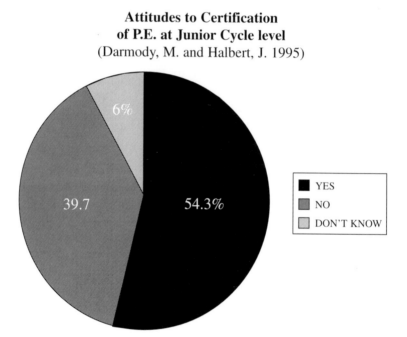

While this survey highlights the fact that the majority of teachers favour certification in the subject, it nevertheless suggests that there exists a very sizable number opposed to such a move. The many arguments for an against certification, according to O'Boyle (1991), can be summarised as follows:

In favour of Certification:

- Certification would provide credibility for the subject and make it comparable to the other academic subjects in our schools.

Against Certification:

- Certification in Physical Education would distort the essential nature of the subject. It does not need academic credibility as it has its own unique contribution to make to the education of our students.

These opposing views were clearly stated at the 1996 AGM of the Physical Education Association of Ireland. However, on this occasion the overwhelming majority of those attending, felt that the time had now arrived for some form of certification in the subject. The Physical Education Association of Ireland adopted a motion stating **"That the subject titled Physical Education be a subject for Certification".**
John Michael Porter, the President of the Physical Education Association of Ireland stated at that time that:

"we must look at the implications of this decision, especially in regard to whether it should be an option or for all, how it can be timetabled in schools and how it will affect the teachers workload and conditions".

Many educationalists subscribe to the view that certification in the subject would help give Physical Education status, and as a result the Physical Education teacher would be in a considerably stronger position to bargain for the much needed resources that he or she requires, but which in some cases, are not made available because of monetary restriction by school authorities. In regard to certification Halbert (1994), is of the opinion that:

"The great concern persists that any subject which remains outside the certification "pale" will experience exaggerated curricular squeeze. Money resources and most importantly pupils will drift to other 'higher status' subjects. If physical education is treated differently in respect of certification there is danger that it will be marginalised . As it is by the time physical education gets into the curriculum in any new form, other subjects will have garnered the lion's share of time and resources. Our subject doesn't need to be any more different."

A great number have yet to be fully convinced that certification alone in Physical Education at Junior Cycle is the best possible answer to enhance the subject from its current state at Junior Cycle. Many believe that every student should experience Physical Education outside the pressure associated with certification, as is so easily seen from other subjects. However, many others subscribe to the view that every student should also have an opportunity to pursue it at certification level, should they so wish.
Accordingly to John Rafferty, Head of the Physical Education Department in the Abbey C.C.S. Grammar School in Newry, Co. Down, 'non-examination'

Physical Education is compulsory for all his students up until the age of 16. This was a result of Article 7 of the Education Reform (Northern Ireland) Order 1989 which

> "places a duty on the Department to set in place by statutory order programmes of study and attainment target for each of the compulsory contributory subjects within the curriculum. Accordingly the Department has made the above Order relating to physical education".

All of Mr Rafferty's students also have an opportunity to study the subject at G.C.S.E. Level should they so wish. It can be strongly argued that every Irish student be offered a similar type choice at Junior Cycle.

A Look Towards the Future - The NCCA Interim Report on Physical Education

In 1994, a Course Committee was set up by the NCCA. Its specific task is clearly defined, as follows; it will

> "advise the NCCA on the structure, format and content of a syllabuses for Physical Education at post-primary level and, also, on issues related to the assessment and certification of pupil progress and achievement in relation to such a syllabus or syllabuses".

On 6th February 1996, the Interim Report on Physical Education was presented to the Council of NCCA, and the Education Officer stated that it was well received. Particular points of interest and concern that arose from this Report included:

(1) the decline in the status and provision of the subject.
(2) the over-emphasis on games in many programmes.
(3) the need to have P.E. included as part of the core curriculum, while accepting that the core is becoming very congested.
(4) the importance of the certification debate.
(5) the increase in the use of non-qualified P.E. teachers, and the desirability of providing adequate numbers of properly trained teachers.
(6) the need to involve the subject in the broader strategic planning process, especially in respect of teacher numbers, staffing policies, provision of facilities.

Framework for Junior Cycle

The NCCA Course Committee for Physical Education at Post Primary Level has, to date, developed a broad framework for a Junior Cycle Physical Education Course, which includes the following areas: Body Management, Athletics Games, Aquatics, Adventure Activities, Aesthetic/Artistic. Issues like assessment procedures, certification and the weighting given to each area, at Junior Cycle, are currently being discussed.

Pilot Project in Physical Education at Junior Cycle

It is envisaged that feasibility work on the joint Department of Education/NCCA pilot project at Junior Cycle will commence this Spring, with the project itself commencing full scale operation at the start of the school year 1997-98.

However, at a special meeting convened for ASTI teachers of the subject on the 6th November last at ASTI House, the following were some of the recommendations put forward which need to be considered, before any implementation of the proposed Pilot Project:

- That the 'tools' to be used for any proposed form of assessment should cater for all levels of student ability.
- That provision of adequate resource materials and equipment will be required in order to teach the subject satisfactorily.
- That inservice courses will be of vital importance prior to any introduction of assessment and/or certification.
- That the selection of schools for the proposed joint NCCA/Dept of Ed. Pilot Project, reflect the wide range of circumstances which exist when teaching the subject.
- That if and when certification is introduced, any changes in work practices for Physical Education teachers be financially or otherwise compensated for.
- That there is need for parents to be properly informed of the enormous value of the subject in the "holistic" education of their child.

Should these recommendations be taken on board, it can be argued that the pilot project provides a tremendous opportunity to examine the potential of Physical Education at Junior Cycle. In so doing it will explore the many methods of assessment, including the ASSIST Project (Assessment in Second Level Teaching in Physical Education), that could be utilised by those who will be directly involved at the 'coal face', and arrive at a form of certification which is both relevant and acceptable to all.

Conclusion

This is indeed a critical and exciting time for Physical Education at Junior Cycle. It appears that radical changes in the subject are about to take place. Many positive forces currently exist, together with a most committed workforce of teachers, to provide much hope for the future of the subject at Junior cycle. However, the reality is that many issues have yet to be resolved, as highlighted by the Minister for Education Niamh Bhreathnach, T.D. at the opening of the National Physical Education Conference in October 1994,

> "If P.E. is to become an integral part of the educational experience for every child, questions of resources, of teacher availability, of timetabling and of certification have to be addressed".

Suffice it to say, Minister, that the time to seriously address these issues has well and truly arrived.

Bhreathnach, N. Official opening speech by the Minister for Education. Journal of the *Physical Educational Association of Ireland*. Volume IV Issue 1. Jan. 1995.

Circular No. 1991/24. The Northern Ireland Curriculum. Physical Education. *Programmes of Study and Attainment Targets*. 1991.

Darmody, M. (1989). "Physical Education in southern region VECs and community and comprehensive schools". *Department of Education Inspectorate Report* (Unpublished).

Darmody, M. and Halbert, J. (1995). *Attitudes to Certification at Junior Cycle* (Unpublished survey).

Deenihan, J. (1990). *A survey of physical education in Irish post-primary schools.* (Unpublished)

Department of Education. *Rules and Programmes for Post Primary Education 1986/87*. Stationery Office, Dublin.

Fisher, D (1995) *European Perspectives on the future of Physical Education*. Paper delivered at the National Physical Education Conference. Limerick.

Halbert, J. (1994) *Physical Education at the Crossroads: the way forward*. Proceedings of the National Physical Education Conference. Physical Education Association of Ireland, Limerick.

Higgins, C. (1992). *Aspirations, realities and possibilities: Physical Education in Irish post-primary schools* (Unpublished paper).

Interim Report from the Physical Education Course Committee, presented to the NCCA Council on 6/2/96.

Landsdowne Market Research. (1996) ASTI Teachers Survey.

O'Boyle, D. (1991). *Examinations in Physical - Should we, can we?* The Secondary Teacher Vol. 20, No. 1, p7.

O'Boyle, D and Ryan, E. (1994). *Survey of 74 Physical Education Teachers who attended Inservice Training in A.S.T.I. House* (unpublished).

PEAI Member Survey (1993). *Summary Report for the Physical Education Association of Ireland* (PEAI), AGM.

Department of Education. Targeting Sporting Change in Ireland (1997). Strategic Plan - *Sport in Ireland 1997-2006 and Beyond.*

White Paper on Education (1995) *Charting our Education Future.* Department of Education.

Information Technology in the Junior Cycle Curriculum

JOHN MULCAHY

Introduction

Information Technology is changing the way we live, the way we learn, the way we work. As educators face the challenge of preparing students for the world of work, further education and leisure, competence and familiarity with IT is a core part of that preparation. This is now widely recognised by all the social partners at national and international level. The European White Paper on Education and Training underlines that "basic training in information technology has therefore become a necessity for European Education Systems" (E.U., 1996). These views are echoed in the IBEC 1996 document 'Social Policy in a Competitive Society' which states that "the achievement of competence and understanding in computer literacy and information technology is a core issue at all levels of the education system" (IBEC,1996). Given the advent of the information society, it would be reasonable to expect that Information Technology would feature largely in the Government's blueprint for the development of Irish education. Yet it is scarcely mentioned in the White Paper. Instead, the White Paper refers cursorily to the need for students, on completion of the Junior Certificate programme, to have acquired competence and understanding in practical skills including computer literacy and information technology. As to how this might be achieved, the White Paper is silent other than to state that Information Technology has been identified for cross-curricular development .

Current Provision at Junior Cycle

A non-examination Computer Studies course is provided within the Junior Certificate programme though it is not examined. It requires students to spend about 70 hours on the programme in the course of the Junior Cycle - i.e. one class a week. In an overcrowded programme struggling to find space for

CPSE and RSE, it is doubtful if that time could be afforded for a subject that is not examined. The NCCA must revise policy for IT in the Junior Cycle.

Course Committees have tried to incorporate developments in IT into subject areas at Junior Cycle level. The Business Studies Syllabus expects that students will be made familiar with Information Technology throughout the course and be given the experience of operating it. In particular, it expects that a student, having completed the course, should be able to use a keyboard effectively and accurately. However, it qualifies this expectation by acknowledging that not all students may have access to the equipment required to complete the practical components of this section.

Barriers to Information Technology

One major barrier to the widespread introduction of IT in schools is the availability of funding. To date funding for providing hardware and software to schools is confined to schools offering the Leaving Certificate Vocational and Leaving Certificate Applied Programmes. There is no separate funding for resourcing I.T. at Junior Cycle. Despite this, a recent ASTI survey showed that 78% of schools had computer rooms while 38% had Internet access. The survey also reported 9% of schools were hindered from offering computer studies by an inadequate pupil/teacher ratio (ASTI Survey on Staffing, Funding & Facilities, 1996). The ASTI has submitted comprehensive proposals for the development of IT in second-level schools to the Minister of Education. These proposals should, in the opinion of the ASTI, be regarded as priorities for the development of IT in second level schools.

Information Technology in Post-Primary Schools: General Observations

A comprehensive review of information technology in Irish schools was conducted by NITEC/DCU for the European Commission in 1992. "New Information Technology in the Irish School System" provides a succinct analysis of the evolution of information technology in schools. The Report noted the following constraints influencing the spread of IT in schools:

- absence of hard data on the extent of the spread of IT in schools due to the decentralised nature of the curriculum and the limited involvement of the Department of Education in policy formulation and the supply of hardware and software in schools.
- absence of coherent Departmental policy for the development of IT in schools
- lack of uniformity of IT hardware and software makes it difficult to provide an accurate account of the level and type of activity taking place in schools

The 1996 Forbairt Report - *Ireland, the Digital Age and the Internet* - includes a survey of 254 post-primary schools which provides factual information on computers in schools:

- the average number of computers per second-level school was 22.
- vocational schools were generally better equipped with an average of 29 computers per school
- girls-only schools were less well-equipped with an average of 16 computers per school
- computers were used mainly for computer studies and in subjects where IT is mandatory e.g. Technical Drawing, Business Studies and other Technical subjects
- common business applications were widely used
- little use was made of instructional software or computer-aided learning

The Report found that the level of physical resources in the school is not itself a good indication of the extent of IT usage across the curriculum. Rather, the development of IT in schools to date has largely depended on the enthusiasm and dedication of individual teachers and Departmental personnel. The report also noted that, despite the survey findings of an average of 22 computers per school, in the majority of schools, computers are not powerful enough to run modern multi-media applications using CD roms. The findings reflect trends in other countries which underline that the availability of IT materials in schools was insufficient to ensure the integration of IT into the curriculum. The latter finding is of particular significance for future IT education policy. The integration is dependent upon the willingness of teachers to use IT as a tool for learning and teaching. This issue was also raised in the 1992 Report by NITEC/DCU.

Key Issues and Opportunities

The ASTI has not carried out research on the development of IT in schools. However, through its various committees and representatives structures and its contacts with teachers in schools, it is kept informed of developments in IT in schools. The Association fully concurs with findings of the aforementioned studies.

The ASTI identifies the key issues as regards the spread of IT in schools as follows:

- need for a coherent policy for the development of IT in schools
- need for investment in IT equipment in schools
- need to look at the implications of IT for schools and the role of the teacher

- need for a major programme of inservice training for teachers
- need for the availability of educational software which is relevant to Irish students.

(1) Need for Coherent Policy

Notwithstanding the major developments in education policy which have taken place in recent years, the area of IT in schools has not been addressed in any coherent manner. While the Department of Education has promoted IT in schools, its approach, in the opinion of the ASTI, is fragmented and not based on long-term policy objectives. Indeed, many Departmental initiatives have emerged as a result of the availability of EU funding or other short-term strategic considerations.

The ASTI believes that the absence of a coherent policy for IT at Departmental level is the major obstacle to the progress in this area. The development of such a policy is now urgent given the impending challenges of the Information Society. The ASTI believes that every student should be IT-literate. At the end of Junior Cycle, they should learn to master simple word-processing programmes and computer applications such as databases and spreadsheets. At Senior Cycle, students should continue to develop their basic skills in using different computer programmes and, where desired, go on to more in-depth studies relating to computer programming and the development of software. In order to achieve this goal of IT-literate school leavers, the Department of Education must, as a matter of urgency, develop a comprehensive policy in this area for immediate implementation. Such policy should be drawn up in consultation with education partners and should not be hedged with provisions such as "resources permitting" as are many excellent proposals in the White Paper.

The ASTI recommends that the following issues be addressed in future policy:
- the definition of the role of IT in the curriculum and in the school
- short-term and long-term goals for the integration of IT into the curriculum
- the implications of the integration of IT into the curriculum for teacher education - both pre-service and inservice
- the availability of IT equipment in schools
- availability of the support services in schools
- the development of software for Irish students

The Department of Education, in its submission to the Information Society Steering Committee, expressed its concern re the imposition of a "grand plan" at national level for the development of IT in schools. The ASTI shares this concern: policies for the development of IT in schools which are top-down tend to have a technical rather than a pedagogical focus and do not make an impact on the teaching profession as a whole. As the experience of other countries has demonstrated, developing a sense of ownership among teachers through local pilot projects is essential if IT is to become an integral part of the school curriculum. However, the ASTI would be concerned that, as has happened in other areas of education policy, in the absence of a national framework, pilot projects on their own do not tend to have a sustained impact at national level - irrespective of the excellence of the individual project. Thus, while bearing in mind the concerns outlined above, the ASTI recommends that the Department of Education develop a national policy framework for IT in the education system, an essential element of which would be the development of relevant pilot projects with dissemination measures clearly delineated. The establishment of a National Technology in Education Unit, as proposed by the Department of Education, which would be representative of the teaching profession, would seem to meet the need for, on the one hand, a co-ordinated approach, and on the other, an approach which is bottom-up and, crucially, which is owned by the teaching profession. In this context the role of the National Information Technology in Education Centre - NITEC - will need to be reviewed. The expertise developed in this Centre constitutes a good foundation for the development of a National Unit. Moreover, the model of curriculum support and innovation developed by the Transition Year Support Team and other senior cycle programme initiatives represents an excellent model for a National Technology in Education Unit.

A National Unit should, inter alia, have responsibility for:

- developing policy for IT in schools and advising the relevant bodies on policy, including the Department of Education, NCCA, NCVA, etc.
- providing inservice to teachers and school staffs
- supporting the development of educational software and resource materials for teachers
- supporting the development of educational software and resource materials for students with disabilities and those who are under-achieving at school
- providing assistance and advice to schools on integrating IT within the curriculum
- providing advice to teachers on opportunities for further education and training in the area of IT
- disseminating information to schools on opportunities for IT development as part of EU and other trans-national school projects

(ii) Integration of I.T. into the curriculum : implications for teachers and classroom practice:

The integration of IT in the school curriculum has very significant implications for the way teaching and learning takes place in our schools. Learning how to learn is increasingly the focus of curriculum reform where the emphasis is on enabling the individual student to realise his/her intellectual potential and to develop his/her specific talents and aptitudes. In this context the role of the teacher is qualitatively different to the standard didactic role. Increasingly, teachers view themselves, and are required by society to function, as educational leaders who facilitate students' learning and who, in turn, are in a learning role themselves. Students' roles are also changing as they are required to develop their own learning skills and engage in an ongoing process of exploration of the rapidly expanding knowledge base. However, all cognitive developments rest on a process of interaction between the teacher and students. Skills, attitudes and values are all encompassed in this cognitive process which can never be usurped by technology. In this respect, teachers should not fear technology: while it will change the way the learning process is managed, it will not undermine their role as education leader. The ASTI believes that it is important that teachers' fears in this respect are taken on board by policy-makers. Nor are these fears unique to the teaching profession.

Within the teaching profession, as within the broader society, there is a great diversity of opinion concerning the merits of widespread usage of IT in all areas of life. The majority of Irish teachers belong to an age group whose educational experiences and professional training preceded the computer age. Many of these teachers work in environments which are not "resource rich" but who, nonetheless, ensure the availability of a quality education service to a greater number of students than ever before. They are not computer literate and are probably not familiar with the potential of IT to enhance the quality of students'' learning experiences and of their own teaching.

Moreover, like the great majority of Irish people of this age group, they may not fully understand the nature and scope of IT and may be apprehensive as to its power to transform familiar activities and institutions.The profile of Irish teachers in this aspect is no different to that of other teaching forces throughout the industrialised world. As is evident from the national and the international research in this area, the success or failure of IT in schools depends on the responsiveness of the teaching force to embrace change. The Department of Education's submission correctly identifies the following factors as being critical to the widespread usage of IT in schools, namely, teachers' attitudes, teachers' pedagogical skills and teachers' IT skills. The ASTI believes that if the proper support structures are put in place, teachers will respond creatively and with enthusiasm to challenge of IT. Support structures should include:

- Access to ongoing inservice education and training in IT. In order to encourage teachers to participate in such training, incentives should be provided in the form of paid educational leave, accreditation of training undertaken, appropriate remuneration for the successful completion of IT training, opportunities for progression in IT education and training.

- Inservice education and training should have as its primary aim that of developing teachers' pedagogical skills using the medium of IT rather than focusing on the acquisition of technical skills per se. Training content should be based on the use of IT as a tool for extending learning opportunities for the student and for the teacher, for introducing the students and teachers to new ways of learning, enhancing the learning opportunities for students who are disadvantaged and those with disabilities, and for supporting innovation in the school curriculum as a whole.

- Making available time to teachers to introduce IT into their teaching practice and to develop suitable programmes for students. Lack of time was acknowledged in the Department of Education's submission as a barrier to the introduction of IT in schools. The pressures on the teachers' working day are enormous and many teachers simply do not have the time to engage in developing IT initiatives in their classroom teaching or as part of their wider professional duties. Schools must have adequate numbers of teachers; school timetables must, by reducing their class contact time, facilitate teachers who wish to develop IT initiatives.

- Positive attitudes from the school management authorities to IT is also a critical factor in promoting IT in schools. The White Paper has elaborated on the role of the school management in promoting change in schools. Specific measures require to be taken to inform school managements of the importance of developing IT in Irish schools and of ensuring that all school leavers are computer literate. The Principal teacher, in particular, has an important role to play in facilitating the introduction of IT in schools and in ensuring that IT becomes an integral feature of the school curriculum. The latter will only come about if the school management has a vision of the type of school it wants and has developed capacities for effecting change in their schools. Principals require support to effect such changes: access to inservice education and training educational leadership should be available on an ongoing basis.

In addition to changing the learning environment for all students, the integration of IT into the school curriculum has untold potential for improving the learning opportunities for students who are disadvantaged as a result of physical or intellectual disabilities or socio-economic background. Because IT presents new ways of learning, it will give disadvantaged students access to the curriculum in a manner appropriate to their level of cognitive development and which reinforces their learning styles and abilities. There are already some excellent initiatives underway in Northern Ireland, for example, in this area whereby students are facilitated to work individually or in teams on computer programmes aimed at improving basic literacy and numeracy skills. The integration of IT into the curriculum also opens up the school to the wider world by allowing for instant communication with students and schools all over the world. Students will be able to communicate with students in other countries, will be able to share information and will be able to engage in joint projects and other learning situations. Indeed, some schools are already well advanced in this respect.

The promotion of the European Dimension in Education, which is so essential to aiding the process of European political integration, requires a proactive approach by schools to the use of IT. Moreover, if some schools are not to miss out completely on availing of opportunities for European educational co-operation, specific measures must be put in place to ensure that all schools have the IT-capacity for meaningful participation in EU programmes for schools.

Links with the local community and industry can also be greatly enhanced through IT. Many schools have already developed various projects of this nature. IBEC has assisted such developments through a specific support programmes to assist school-industry partnerships. The ASTI believes that all schools should be involved in such partnership.

The development of IT in schools has particular significance for small schools and rural schools. One-third of all secondary schools have student enrolments of 300 students or less. Departmental staffing regulations are a major barrier to the provision of a balanced curriculum, suitable for all ability levels. IT can play a major roles in enhancing the curriculum in these schools by enabling students to participate in distance learning activities.

Within the broader school context, IT can contribute to making school administration more efficient through the development of efficient databases, computerised timetabling, efficient record keeping, etc. It can also assist teachers in the planning and preparation of work for their students and the work attendant upon their other responsibilities as Year Heads, Programme Co-Ordinators, Holders of Posts of Responsibility, etc.

(iii) Availability of Suitable Hardware and Software

The availability of IT hardware in schools is, as has been demonstrated at home and abroad, no guarantee that IT will be successfully integrated into the curriculum. The latter depends on the ability of the teaching force to utilise the IT and to use it as part of their daily teaching. Nonetheless, the issue of the availability of suitable hardware and software in schools is a critical factor in ensuring that IT is utilised as a pedagogic tool in all areas of the curriculum. Both the NITEC/DCU and Forbairt Reports identified unsuitable hardware and software as one of the key factors hindering the willingness of teachers to get involved in using IT outside subject areas where computer applications are required. The Reports found that a considerable proportion of the hardware in schools was not suitable for adaptation to information networks or for multi-media activities thereby undermining the idea of the computer as an aid to learning in a variety of subject areas. Investment must be made to upgrade computer facilities in schools to ensure that the full potential of IT can be realised in the school. The Department of Education or the National Technology in Education Unit should develop guidelines for minimum standards for IT equipment in schools and should provide technical advice and assistance to schools when purchasing technology.

The Reports also noted that many teachers did not use educational software not because they were unable to use such packages but, rather, because they did not consider many of the available software packages as being relevant to the aims of the syllabus or the curriculum. Reports from the European Commission have also identified the non-availability of suitable educational software as a factor inhibiting the use of IT by teachers. The availability of educational software suitable for use in Irish schools must be considered as a priority if teachers are to make greater use IT in their classroom teaching. Teachers should be actively involved in the development of the educational software and appropriate measures should be put in place to facilitate teachers' involvement in this area such as paid educational leave and teacher secondment.

All schools should be provided with technical assistants on site to provide teachers and students with advice and assistance in the usage of IT. Technical assistants should also be responsible for the maintenance of IT equipment in schools and for helping teachers to develop school-based software for use in the classroom and in school administration.

(iv) Investment in Information Technology in Schools

Technological change is the most dynamic force for change in our societies today. The communications and information revolution is already transforming our everyday lives. Consequently, computer literacy must be regarded as inseparable from literacy in general. As a minimum, society expects schools to provide our young people with the forms of literacy necessary for survival in the modern economy. Inevitably, the responsibilities for achieving mass technological literacy will rest with schools. As noted in the Departmental Submission, many developed countries have specifically targeted the education system as the priority area for implementing overall national IT strategy.

It is imperative for the well-being of society that schools are not left behind in the technological revolution. If the education system is perceived to be falling behind in the information society, schools will be marginalised. Such a development would have very serious implication in terms of the public's attitudes to schools and to education systems more generally. It is essential that investment in IT in the education system takes place within the context of coherent policy objectives and is system-wide. Every single school in the country should have the facilities to make the integration of IT in the curriculum a reality. Specifically, schools should have adequate numbers of computers, low cost access to the Internet and appropriate software. Schools should be not expected to fund their IT out of their standard capitation or budgetary allocation. Rather, a specific annual grant should be made available to schools based on student enrolment for the development of IT in the curriculum. A comprehensive training programme for teachers will have to be put in place if policy objectives are to be achieved. Investment policy for IT in schools will also have to take on board the issue of inequalities in funding in our schools and of the needs of disadvantaged students who come from homes which are not technology rich and which do not have the positive attitudes to learning and education which are so essential to children's achievement at school. Existing social and economic inequalities will be exacerbated if a "two-tier" system of technology-rich and technology-poor schools is allowed to emerge. Investment policy will also have to take cognisance of the gaps that currently exist in terms of male and female students' access to technological subjects. The consequences of such gender-gaps for participation in the labour market have already been well documented.

Conclusion

The second-level education system must respond quickly and systematically to the challenges of the Information Society. It must be enabled to do so through increased investment, financial investment in schools, teacher inservice training, the availability of hardware and software and the development of a National Technology in Education Unit. The integration of IT in the curriculum is achievable if a genuine commitment exists at Government level ensuring that, as we approach the end of the millennium, every school leaver is computer literate.

THE JUNIOR CERTIFICATE ELEMENTARY PROGRAMME: A FRAMEWORK FOR CHANGE IN THE JUNIOR CYCLE

AIDEEN CASSIDY

The Junior Certificate Elementary Programme (JCEP) is one of the latest innovations in the Irish education system and its national implementation was announced in August 1996 by the Minister of Education, Niamh Bhreathnach. The aim of the programme is to provide an alternative approach to the Junior Certificate Programme, specifically aimed at those young people who show signs of school failure or early leaving. The National and Social Forum Report, 1997, *Early School Leavers and Youth Unemployment,* found that 3,200 left school before the Junior Certificate Programme in 1995 and a further 2,400 failed to get at least five passes in that examination[1]. The experience of school is one of failure and alienation for many of these students. The JCEP is an intervention into the Junior Certificate Programme, designed to ensure that these young people can benefit from their time in school through acknowledging and rewarding their achievements. It is targeted at schools with a serious problem in early school leaving. At present, 45 schools and centres offer the programme and a further 15 will be involved in the next academic year with a total of 80 schools by 1999.

The programme has strong foundations, with its origins in the Early School Leavers Project (1979-87) and the School Certificate Programme Pilot Network (1987-96), of the Curriculum Development Unit (CDU)[2].

The definition of early school leavers submitted by the CDU to the Commission of European Communities in 1979 reads as follows :

Those students who derive little or no benefit from their schooling, who leave school at the earliest opportunity, who are unfit for the world of work and consequently drift from one job to another or remain more or less permanently unemployed.[3]

Recent trends show that such students are remaining in school longer because the traditional dead end jobs they tended to drift into are more difficult to find today. Their experience of school is still, however, often negative and their examination prospects are usually poor.

Faced with the difficulties of teaching these students, a group of committed teachers, untrained for the task and within an education system which was failing both teachers and these students, set about developing a new approach. These teachers found that the lack of structures to acknowledge success (outside of the examination), coupled with the students' lack of belief in themselves and their expectation of continued failure were at the root of the problem.

The focus, therefore, of their approach was the needs of the individual pupil. They aimed to break the cycle of failure by certifying what the pupils could do rather than highlighting what they could not. The emphasis was on the positive and the avoidance of self defeating negativity.

The first step in establishing the needs of the individual is to recognise the reasons for their failure and so it may be useful to consider the major motivating factors for successful students. We would suggest that they would include the following :

- a supportive home background;
- confidence in their ability to succeed in the examination system;
- peer pressure to succeed;
- a sense of building their own future;
- a wish to conform and belong to the educational mainstream;
- a sense of satisfaction from their achievements;
- an interest in the subject;

The JCEP is aimed at pupils who lack most, if not all, of these motivating factors. These are students of whom it has been said: "Schooling has left them no tangible reward nor in many cases nothing more than a minimal level of competence" [4]

They often present themselves in two ways:

- unruly, uninterested and from many teachers' perspective,undesirable,
- very quiet, withdrawn and uninvolved.

The latter usually drift away from school - each missed school day, often backed up by parental support, compounding the problem. Absence causes them to be educationally backward and socially poorly adjusted. Poor attainment and the lack of friends on return to school form the vicious circle leading to drop out.[5]

The departure of the former is likely to be somewhat more spectacular. Understandably, many hard pressed teachers do not mourn the loss of these children, and practise " tactical tolerance of their disappearance".[6]

Unfortunately, for the children involved and society in general, the consequences of this system failure can be profound. Report after report highlight the link between poverty, disadvantage, crime and youth unemployment and early school leaving. Gary Granville has pointed out that the well educated students face unemployment and so the needs of the non-exam students are far down the list. These are the most serious victims of unemployment.[7] This view is borne out in the findings of the Forum report which makes many recommendations to tackle the problem, including intervention at pre-school, primary, secondary and beyond. It is in this context that the JCEP should be seen, as part of a nationwide effort to solve the problem of early leaving.

It could be said that our present examination system aggravates the problem, in that it is designed to reward excellence and ensure failure. Eurydice in their summary analysis of *Measures to Combat School Failure: A Challenge for Europe,* describes it as 'a culture of excellence',[8] where excellence has value only if not accessible to all. A culture of failure is an essential part of the present system, and it exists to prove the value of the successful. In our view, this approach to education is both flawed and unfair.

Teachers are pressurised by the examination system, particularly in schools where results are the measure of a good teacher. This pressure can force teachers to forget about good practice and concentrate on getting the motivated student through the examination. Teachers can therefore feel professionally threatened by students who are at risk of failure and consequently experience a sense of helplessness and isolation.

In Service Needs

Eurydice found that most teachers have little knowledge of the techniques of formative assessment and the strategies of differentiated education. Many teachers still consider their task to be the transmission of knowledge, whereas they are increasingly expected to be not only subject specialists but also teaching specialists. They consider in-service training for teachers to be still too frequently limited to updating teachers' knowledge of their own subjects.[9]

Teachers need more training. Traditional teaching methods can be very successful when one is dealing with well motivated students but often fail when dealing with unreceptive students. Indeed, teachers sometimes perceive themselves as the failures when traditional methods prove ineffective. This sense of failure can be a huge source of stress. Teachers need a framework to develop new strategies. Without such a framework schools will continue to squeeze these students out, because there is no room for them in an entirely examination driven class.

We would argue that it is possible to meet the needs of our failing students, even in the present, examination dominated, school system. Furthermore, we are convinced that by the development of new strategies we can make the education experience more rewarding and much less stressful for many pupils and teachers.

We fully endorse the recommendations of the Eurydice Report which states that the goal of a good education should be: "to stimulate the greatest number to learn as much as possible."[10] The report suggests that good teaching practice should include two aspects:

a) a feedback - aspect which would permit the pupil to assess what has been learned in relation to the objectives to be attained;

b) a guidance aspect which would enable teaching to be adjusted or redirected more appropriately towards mastery of skills in question.[11]

The JCEP provides a framework and offers an 'education for success' which all students and teachers deserve.

The Curriculum

The content of the curriculum is based on the Junior Certificate syllabuses but extends the range of knowledge and skills, ensuring that the students can gain credit for a wider range of achievements than those included in terminal examination. Included are the following:

• Basic concept and skills are explicitly stated which are essential for the student's progress in whole curriculum. These concepts and skills are often only implied in the Junior Certificate syllabuses. They include, but are not confined to, literacy and numeracy.

• Personal and social development, which includes life-skills, relationships, and self esteem.

In addition all students must follow courses leading to the foundation level in English and mathematics, and also follow a suitable course in Irish. Other suitable subjects are included on the timetable based on the students' needs, ideally following a process of early identification of those needs.

The student profile system consists of a series of learning targets or statements the student can work towards, which provides the basis for the process of curriculum planning, monitoring, recording and feedback.[12] The profile provides an individualised record of achievement which the student has demonstrated over a period of time. Each statement describes a skill, concept or area of knowledge affirming that the student can do something, knows or understands something. There is a bank of subject centred and cross-curricular statements which teachers can choose from. Each statement is broken down into a series of short-term achievable goals.

Planning is a vital aspect of the curriculum which has proved very useful for teachers, as the profiling system provides a ready made framework for planning out a programme tailor made to meet the needs of the students in the context of the Junior Certificate. Teachers choose statements to work towards with a group, only if they deem them to be achievable, based on a comprehensive picture of the child's ability and the nature of the difficulties.

The development of links with the primary school to facilitate early identification of difficulties is very important. *The Report Of The Pupil Transfer Committee,*[13] points out that many pupils cannot cope with the change second level brings, often leading to their leaving school. The recommendations of their report are very similar to the aims and aspirations of the JCEP, ideally building a bridge between the child centred, integrated curriculum of the primary school and that of second level.

Positive feedback with regard to progress on each statement is central. Students are aware of the aims for the term and year. They understand that all their work will count towards their achieving each statement. The possibilities of achieving each objective is highlighted, and shown to be a stepping stone towards success in the Junior Certificate examination. One of the principal aims of the programme is that the students gain confidence through regular positive feedback and so develop a much more productive attitude towards school, ultimately leading to their sitting the Junior Certificate examination.

The framework provides an opportunity for ongoing feedback to parents which, for some may be the first positive contact with school. Parents are encouraged to support the efforts of their children. There is no doubt that active parental involvement is hugely helpful in keeping a child in school.

Finally, the culmination of the curriculum is a folder containing 'a standardized document, agreed by the individual school authorities and validated by the Department of Education which describes the knowledge, skills and achievements which their students have attained'.[14]

On leaving school those students who have been profiled for a minimum of one school year will receive a certification folder containing:

- A Junior Certificate (where applicable);
- A certificate attesting to the student's satisfactory completion of the Junior Certificate Elementary Programme;
- Individualised student profile listing statements achieved and;
- A reference from the school authorities.

Teaching Strategies

The teaching methods which are promoted in the JCEP are experiential, interactive, relevant, systematic and structured. The students actively learn by doing rather than through teacher demonstration. Students and teachers work together with a sense of common purpose. Topics are set in a meaningful context which the students can relate to in their own lives. Content is made relevant to the young people's age and interest level. All learning, especially literacy and numeracy, is taught in a structured and systematic way following set goals.

Cross-curricular work reinforces learning across subject boundaries while, continuing, to some extent, the integrated work of the primary school. Cross-curricular work also promotes team work among the teachers. Teachers work together on cross-curricular statements which focus on skills and knowledge common to many subjects. All teachers have the potential to contribute to what is arguably the most important aspect of the curriculum, personal and social development, which enhances self-esteem and the ability to relate well to people. The teachers, through the JCEP framework are afforded the time to meet to develop these cross curricular links. At present some teams are working on cross curricular projects, or are focusing on agreed interdisciplinary topics. This team work is very fruitful as the pupils benefit from consistency and the teachers benefit from the support and the opportunity to share ideas. Additionally, the subject teachers get an opportunity to view the students' education as a whole, to see them as individuals, not simply maths or woodwork students. The students' performance may them be viewed more globally by each teacher and by the school authorities. If the student stays in school, that is acknowledged as success and each teacher may view him/herself as a contributor in a meaningful way over the years to that success. Adoption of a cross-curricular teaching strategy has proved very successful in the current network of schools and there is great scope for its further development with the help of in-service training.

I can personally testify to the effectiveness of the teaching approach which underpins the JCEP. I acted as coordinator of the Junior Certificate Elementary

Programme in Jobstown Community College for several years. Jobstown is a disadvantaged area in West Tallaght in Dublin with unemployment over 70%, and the school experiences a very serious drop out rate. The programme was offered to the two groups in most need of remediation. The classes were usually made up of students with behaviour/emotional problems, and learning difficulties. Many of these students were educationally unmotivated, withdrawn and some had special needs. Usually a class of 16 starting in first year would on average have 8 students or less remaining in third year. With the help of the programme and all the support structures that were linked with it (i.e.tutor system, year head, home school community liaison officer, remedial teacher and strong links with the primary schools) we had many successes. The most recent example was a class which enrolled in 1994, 18 pupils in all. 16 of those sat their Junior Certificate very successfully in 1996. The majority are now involved in Transition Year, Leaving Certificate or Leaving Certificate Applied and are reportedly doing very well.

The strengths of the programme were the acknowledgment of the intrinsic worth of the individual, the celebration and nurturing of their strengths, whatever they were, and the encouragement experienced by the pupils from each achievement. The end result was that the students believed in themselves - the key to success.

The Future

For too long we have relied on the goodwill and commitment of teachers to help failing students within an unsuitable system and with inadequate resources. Committed teachers will always be an essential ingredient of a successful educational programme, but first teachers should be fully supported and provided with proper training in strategies for coping with these students. Teachers can have a huge influence on a child's future given the proper framework.

Support structures have been put in place at the Curriculum Development Unit for schools offering the programme. Support includes school visits, co-ordinators' meetings and an in-service programme - national, regional and school based. Participating schools are also entitled to an enhanced capitation and improved teacher allocation (to allow time for a co-ordinator and the necessary meetings).

We are evolving from a 'whole school' to a 'whole system' approach to education now that the Department of Education is recognising the value of such programmes and is willing to provide resources to support and train teachers in their efforts. If school authorities embrace this opportunity and actively support the intervention then we, in the education community, can proudly say that we are striving to fulfil our obligation; to cherish all the children of the state equally.

1   The National Economic and Social Forum (1997) *Early School Leavers and Youth Unemployment,* Report No:11, January, p39.
2   The Curriculum Development Unit, Sundrive Road, Crumlin, Dublin, is under the auspices of the City of Dublin Vocational Education Committee.
3   Curriculum Development Unit, (1979)*Report on Early School Leavers,* Submission to the Commission of European Communities.
4   Gary Granville, (1982), *The Work of the Early School Leavers Project,* Compass Vol. 11 No.1 1982, p21
5   David Galloway, (1976), *Persistent Unjustified Absence From School,* Trends Journal, Vol.4, p23.
6   Gary Granville, *The Work of The Early School Leavers Project,* p21
7   Ibid. p11
8   Eurydice, Commission of the Eurpean Communities, (1993), *Measures to Combat School Failure : A Challenge for the Construction of Europe,* Summary Analysis, p16.
9   Ibid., p.12
10 Ibid., p.12
11 Ibid., p.12
12 Department of Education, National Council for Curriculum and Assessment, (1996) *The Junior Certificate Elementary Programme, Guidlelines for schools, p.6.*
13 Government of Ireland, (1981), *Report of the Pupil Transfer Committee,* The Stationery Office, Dublin.
14 *Junior Certificate Elementary Programme,Guidelines For Schools, p.7.*
15 *Ibid., p.6.*

THE CONTRIBUTORS

Áine Hyland is Professor of Education in University College Cork.

Pádraig Breathnach is a teacher in the High School Carrickmacross and has completed a PhD on issues relating to the introduction of the Junior Certificate.

David Tuohy is a lecturer in Education in UCD and has conducted seminars for Principal teachers as part of the ASTI Inservice programme funded by the Incareer Development Unit of the Department of Education.

Jim Callan is a lecturer in education in St. Patrick's College, Maynooth and the author of *Schools for Active Learning.*

Joan Hanafin is a lecturer in the Education Department, University College, Cork.

Mary Duggan is a member of the CEC of the ASTI and a member of the ASTI Equality Committee. She is a teacher in Sacred Heart Ballyshannon.

Carmel Heneghan is a member of the ASTI Equality Committee and a teacher in Ballinrobe Community School, Co. Mayo.

Michael Shevlin represented the ASTI on the Special Education Review Committee. He is now a lecturer in education in Trinity College.

Anne O'Brien is a teacher in Presentation Secondary School in Wexford.

Aileen O'Gorman is a teacher in Presentation Secondary School, Ballyphehane, Cork.

Pat Sexton is a member of the Parents' Council of Tullamore CBS

Imelda Bonel-Elliott is a lecturer and Head of Department in Université du Littoral, Boulogne, France.

Tom Mullins is the NCCA Education Officer for English. He is a lecturer in Education in UCC.

Joe Coy is a teacher in Tuam CBS.

James O'Donoghue is a teacher in Thurles CBS.

Kenneth Milne represents the Church of Ireland Board of Education on the NCCA.

Catherine Fitzpatrick is a member of the CEC and of the ASTI Education Committee. She is a teacher in Patrician Academy, Mallow, Co. Cork.

John Mulcahy is President of the ASTI 1996/97. He is a teacher in Bishopstown Community School, Cork.

Michael O'Bradaigh is a teacher in Colaiste an Spioraid Naomh, Bishopstown.

Michael Stokes is a teacher in Castlecomer Community School and is ASTI Convenor for Civic, Social and Political Education.

Aideen Cassidy is co-ordinator of the Support Service for the Junior Certificate Elementary Programme.

Denis O'Boyle is a teacher in St. Colman's College, Clarmorris. He is ASTI Convenor for Physical Education and is a member of the ASTI Education Committee.

FINANCIAL SERVICES FOR ASTI MEMBERS

MIDAS
Helps you take control of your finances.

CARPLAN
Quality group motor insurance scheme for members and their spouses.

HOMEPLAN
Low cost house insurance...with extra benefits.

MORTGAGE ADVISORY SERVICE
Expert advice on where to get the best mortgage deal.

TAX EFFICIENT SAVINGS PROGRAMMES
Investing profitably in your future.

SERIOUS ILLNESS PROTECTION PLAN
A cash lump sum should you suffer a specified serious illness.

SALARY PROTECTION SCHEME
Guarantees you an income in the event of disability.

ADDITIONAL VOLUNTARY CONTRIBUTIONS
To augment benefits under the Superannuation Scheme
for those who have missed years of service.

INVESTMENT ADVICE
Independent advice on where to invest your money.

WOODCHESTER BROKERS,
Dublin: Christchurch Square, Dublin 8. Tel: (01) 408 4000
Cork: Woodchester House, Lr. Glanmire Rd., Cork. Tel: (021) 502 444
Galway: Ard Rí House, Lr. Abbeygate Street, Galway. Tel: (091) 562 727